# Cambridge Elements ≡

Elements in Ancient Egypt in Context
edited by
Gianluca Miniaci
*University of Pisa*
Juan Carlos Moreno García
*CNRS, Paris*
Anna Stevens
*University of Cambridge and Monash University*

# ANCIENT EGYPT IN ITS AFRICAN CONTEXT

## *Economic Networks, Social and Cultural Interactions*

Andrea Manzo
*University of Naples 'L'Orientale'*

**CAMBRIDGE**
UNIVERSITY PRESS

# CAMBRIDGE
## UNIVERSITY PRESS

University Printing House, Cambridge CB2 8BS, United Kingdom

One Liberty Plaza, 20th Floor, New York, NY 10006, USA

477 Williamstown Road, Port Melbourne, VIC 3207, Australia

314–321, 3rd Floor, Plot 3, Splendor Forum, Jasola District Centre,
New Delhi – 110025, India

103 Penang Road, #05–06/07, Visioncrest Commercial, Singapore 238467

Cambridge University Press is part of the University of Cambridge.

It furthers the University's mission by disseminating knowledge in the pursuit of
education, learning, and research at the highest international levels of excellence.

www.cambridge.org
Information on this title: www.cambridge.org/9781009074544
DOI: 10.1017/9781009070638

First published 2022

*A catalogue record for this publication is available from the British Library.*

ISBN 978-1-009-07454-4 Paperback
ISSN 2516-4813 (online)
ISSN 2516-4805 (print)

# Ancient Egypt in Its African Context

## Economic Networks, Social and Cultural Interactions

Elements in Ancient Egypt in Context

DOI: 10.1017/9781009070638
First published online: March 2022

Andrea Manzo
*University of Naples 'L'Orientale'*
**Author for correspondence:** Andrea Manzo, amanzo@unior.it

**Abstract:** This Element discusses the relations between Egypt and its African neighbours. In the first section, the history of studies, the different kind of sources available on the issue and a short outline of the environmental setting are provided. In the second section, the relations between Egypt and its African neighbours from the late Prehistory to Late Antique times are summarized. In the third section, the different kinds of interactions are described, as well as their effects on the lives of individuals and groups, and the related cultural dynamics such as selection, adoption, entanglement and identity building. Finally, the possible future perspective of research on the issue is outlined, both in terms of methods, strategies, themes and specific topics, and of regions and sites whose exploration promises to provide a crucial contribution to the study of the relations between Egypt and Africa.

This Element also has a video abstract: www.cambridge.org/manzo

**Keywords:** Ancient Egypt, Africa, trade, interactions, entanglement

ISBNs: 9781009074544 (PB), 9781009070638 (OC)
ISSNs: 2516-4813 (online), 2516-4805 (print)

# Contents

# 1 Introduction

## 1.1 Egypt and Africa: A Debated Issue

Since the beginning of research into ancient Egypt the issue of its relations with the rest of Africa has been a constantly debated subject. It is well known that the Nile runs through Egypt, constituting its lifeblood, yet this river originates in Africa, a fact that has produced constant speculation on relations with the upstream regions. This debate on Egyptian–African relations is not only embedded in the geographical setting itself, but is also tied up with the origins of Egyptology and with the general cultural milieu of nineteenth and twentieth century Europe. It should be remarked that in the earliest studies on the cultures of the Nile valley, scholars were heavily conditioned by the ideas and theories elaborated by ancient writers. In particular, as far as this specific issue is concerned, Diodorus Siculus, a Greek author, suggested that several Egyptian religious features may have had a southern, or what he termed 'Ethiopian', origin (Diodorus Siculus *Bib. Hist.* III, 2, 3). For this reason, it was initially believed that the Meroitic remains of Nubia may have pre-dated Egyptian dynastic antiquities. Such a view arose after Mohammed Ali khedive of Egypt had conquered the regions South of the First Cataract in 1820, and the rich archaeological heritage of Nubia was revealed to Westerners (Trigger 1994: 325). However, after his first scientific expedition to record the monuments in the Middle Nile area (Lepsius 1849), Karl Richard Lepsius demonstrated that the Napatan and Meroitic remains were contemporary to the latest phases of Egyptian dynastic history and most of the Egyptian remains of the region could not be dated earlier than the New Kingdom.

After this first phase, also based on physical anthropological evidence, the origins of dynastic Egypt were placed within a broad Hamitic horizon characterizing several regions of Africa. Yet, these Hamites were not regarded as autochthonous, but were considered to have originated from migratory movements into the continent (Reid 2003: 65–6). Indeed, the general cultural and political atmosphere characterizing the West during the early twentieth century was deeply affected by colonialism and racial prejudice. Such preconceptions made it difficult to accept that the elaborate Egyptian dynastic culture may have originated from a local (i.e. African) background. Even William Flinders Petrie, the founder of Predynastic studies and an early expert on the emergence of the Egyptian civilization, was no stranger to such views. He believed that the origins of Egypt lay in subsequent migrations from Europe and Asia, whose cultural effects were sometimes disrupted precisely by Nubian (i.e. African) invasions, invariably leading to phases of regression (Petrie 1920: 47–9). Junker's suggestion that the earliest inhabitants of the Neolithic villages in

Lower Egypt may have originated in Libya did little to challenge the then dominant view that the origins of dynastic Egypt were not African, as the peoples of early Libya were considered of Aryan origin (Voos 2016: 222–5).

This inherently colonialist approach is also evident in the interpretations of the cultural trajectories south of the First Cataract provided by George Andrew Reisner, the father of Nubian archaeology. In his view, the phases of cultural dynamism in Nubian history were largely dependent on the arrival of groups from the north (i.e. Egypt), while he invariably ascribed the phases of decline to a prevailing southern or local-indigenous (i.e. African) component (Trigger 1994: 331). This interpretation also relied heavily on the prevalent assumptions held by comparative anatomists in the first part of the twentieth century (Adams 1977: 91–2). Indeed, Reisner's interpretation of the site of Kerma is clearly emblematic: not only did he regard the site, which is characterized by the remains of monumental architectural complexes, as an Egyptian outpost in Nubia (Reisner 1923b: 542–3, 554–5), but he also outlined a trajectory of decline to explain its ultimate end and abandonment (Figure 1). He related this regression to the ethnic prevalence of African components over Egyptian ones (Reisner 1923b: 556–9). Of course, today we know that the site of Kerma was the main centre of the Nubian kingdom, which was the partner as well as

**Figure 1** The Western Deffufa at Kerma, a temple of the local Kerma culture, thought by Reisner to be an Egyptian fortress (© Mission Suisse-Franco-Soudanaise de Kerma/Doukki Gel).

competitor of Egypt in the Nile valley from the second half of the third to the mid-second millennium BC (Sections 2.2 and 2.3). However, it took a long time for the general perspective to change: for a considerable period of time the archaeology of the regions south of Egypt indeed remained the archaeology of the Egyptian frontier (Edwards 2004: 7–9).

This view continued to dominate even after the Second World War. It portrayed Egypt's African neighbours as culturally passive actors in an asymmetrical relationship. Indeed, the Nubians were deemed to be dependent on Egypt for all forms of cultural and technological innovation. A real change in how scholarship understood Egyptian–African relations only took place in the more general context of the decolonization. The new African nations were eager to identify their historical roots and for this reason were highly interested in ancient history and archaeology. At that time, a debate began not only on the active role that Africans had in history, but also on the African roots of Egypt itself (O'Connor & Reid 2003: 7–8). In the specific case of Nubia, this debate involved scholars who had taken part in the final salvage campaign of the monuments of Lower Nubia started in 1960. These scholars certainly helped to bring a different perspective to the debate. Indeed, the colonial paradigm largely followed the view of the African peoples that emerged from ancient Egyptian texts (Adams 1977: 88–90, Török 1997: 20–2), while many of these scholars came to study Nubia via backgrounds that were not Egyptology. The extent to which early interpretations of the relationship between Africa and Egypt were re-evaluated is evident in the debate that followed the discoveries in the A-Group elite Cemetery L at Qustul. The identification in the remains at Qustul of locally made objects decorated with iconographies similar to the royal representations and symbols in Egypt and that were potentially earlier than Egyptian ones, led to the conclusion that they were the archetypes that inspired the Egyptian ones (Williams 1986: 139–47, but see Section 3.3) (Figure 2). In the meantime, Egypt was not only regarded as the oldest civilization in Africa, but also as the intermediary through which African civilization profoundly influenced the cultures of the Mediterranean and Europe (O'Connor & Reid 2003: 7–8). Moreover, as a reaction against the earlier interpretations, the Egyptian influence on its African neighbours was now considered marginal if not non-existent, and the cultural changes occurring in those regions were almost exclusively explained by internal socio-cultural or environmental factors (Trigger 1994: 336–8).

Of course, if the intensity and the complexity of the interactions between Egypt and its African neighbours is considered (see Sections 2 and 3), this narrative is also far from satisfactory, and for this reason a more balanced approach came to emerge. This understanding has largely been based on the

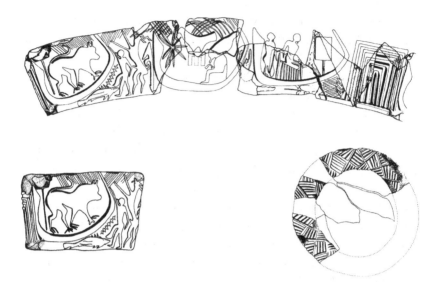

**Figure 2** A stone incense burner from Qustul L Cemetery, decorated with iconographies also characterizing the earliest royal monuments in Egypt (© Oriental Institute of the University of Chicago).

anthropological concept of entanglement. This concept has been adopted to study the interaction between the Nubian and Egyptian cultures and it recognizes the active role of both components (Smith 2014: 2; Section 3.3). In the meantime, the awareness also emerged in Nubian studies that there was a local function and a meaning given to borrowed cultural elements, whether originating in Egypt or elsewhere, and this was crucial to achieving a more nuanced understanding of cross-cultural interaction (Török 2009: xvi; 2018: 2). More recent studies on the Egyptian side of this interaction have pointed out the relevance of African elements to the rise of Egyptian culture (see Sections 2.1 and 3.3), following earlier suggestions on Egyptian kingship and religion by Henri Frankfort (1948; see also Cervelló Autori 1996). Moreover, African contributions to the later phases of Egyptian history can certainly be detected as well (Section 3.3). This counterbalances the traditional view that considers Egypt more closely linked to the Near East than to the rest of Africa (see Smith 2018: 327, 330).

## 1.2 Environmental Setting

The environmental setting of north-eastern Africa certainly played a role in the relations between Egypt and its neighbours. For this reason, it is worthwhile providing a general overview on the whole macro-region here, including the

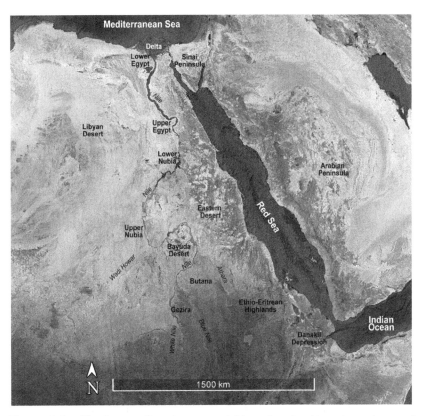

**Figure 3** Satellite image of north-eastern Africa, showing its main regions and features (Google Earth).

ecological zones characterizing it as well as its topographical and hydrological features (Figure 3). Moreover, it should be stressed that this should not be regarded as a static context, as it was obviously affected by the changes that occurred on a global scale. The humid conditions emerging at the end of the Pleistocene continued up until the first half of the Holocene, when drier conditions progressively emerged. These drier conditions were more precociously felt in the northern regions (i.e. in the regions closer to Egypt and in Egypt itself), while the process was slower in more southern areas, where more humid conditions persisted until the end of the second millennium BC (Gatto & Zerboni 2015: 306–12; Riemer & Kindermann 2019: 197).

In general, the Holocene climatic dynamics emphasized the contrast between the Nile valley and its hinterland. The whole region is focussed on the Nile valley, which, as its axis, runs south to north. The natural riches of this river valley included water, land, animal and vegetal resources. The Nile valley is affected by the annual summer flood that originates from the seasonal rains in the Lake Victoria basin and, even more so, from the Ethio-Eritrean highlands. Even to this day the riverine environment contrasts with the hinterland, yet this contrast came to prominence after the emergence of drier conditions from the mid-Holocene onwards. At that time, the available resources in the areas away from the river dramatically decreased, with the only notable exception being the oases in the Western Desert (Dumont 2009: 2–4; Riemer & Kindermann 2019: 195–6). It should be stressed that the very different ecological environments characterizing the valley and the hinterland favoured the economic interdependence between the two, which become increasingly evident in the drier setting of the second half of the Holocene (Gatto & Zerboni 2015: 317). The contrast between the Nile valley and the hinterlands is also evident in the southern fringes of the macro-region. However, it is somehow mitigated in the south by the belt of the tropical monsoons that result in the presence of vast steppes that occur seasonally, re-flourishing at some distance away from the river. The conditions become increasingly humid as we proceed towards the steep edge of the Ethio-Eritrean plateau, where the Blue Nile and the Atbara originate (Dumont 2009: 7). It should be stressed that with some scattered isolated granite or sandstone inselbergs, the Ethio-Eritrean plateau is not the only topographically relevant feature in the macro-region. Indeed, the Eastern Desert is very different from the mostly plain areas that mark the Western Desert, as it is characterized by hilly terrain: the Red Sea hills are crossed by deep valleys of dried up rivers oriented towards the Nile river or alternatively towards the Red Sea. The diversity of the inland areas produces further different ecological niches and concur to the environmental variety in the macro-region.

Over a long period of time, this environmental setting favoured the emergence of permanent settlements in the river valley and in the nearby regions, characterized by a considerable availability of resources all year round. These settlements became inhabited by agro-pastoral groups from a certain point onwards (Gatto & Zerboni 2015: 317). In contrast, the inland areas are characterized by a much lower concentration of resources and by higher seasonal variability in their availability. Consequently, the inland regions were mainly inhabited by more mobile groups, who from a certain point onwards were typically herders (Gatto & Zerboni 2015: 317). The ecological and seasonal contrasts, the economic interdependence between the different areas on one side, and the more general climatic changes on the other since the very beginning encouraged migrations and movements of people, which were also related to economic exchanges and cultural interaction. Indeed, while seasonal environmental variability may have fostered temporary cyclical movements every year, long-term climatic changes may have encouraged bigger and more permanent phenomena such as migrations.

The inherently high degree of connectivity characterizing north-eastern Africa resulting from these environmental factors was enhanced, at least from the fourth millennium BC onwards, by an increasing interest in some of the mineral, animal and vegetal resources that widely occur in the macro-region (Figure 4; Section 2.1). In particular, the presence of highly sought-after commodities was a driving factor behind the increased connectivity. Gold sources characterize the Eastern Desert of Upper Egypt and Nubia up to the north-western Ethio-Eritrean highlands and other gold-bearing areas also occur in the western regions of the highlands themselves (Manzo 1999: 8–9). Noteworthy also are the naturally occurring associations of gold and silver in some of those gold-bearing areas originating an alloy called electrum, while sources of pure silver are absent. Sources of obsidian, a glass-like stone which was highly appreciated for the sharp edges it produces when flaked and was exploited for the production of lithic tools from the prehistoric phases, are located on the Eritrean coast and in the Danakil depression nearby (Espinel 2011: 125; Manzo 1999: 9). This very special type of stone from the African (and Arabian) regions bordering the southern Red Sea continued to be used for producing high-quality luxury objects up until Roman times. In addition to these mineral resources, other commodities could be obtained in the southern sectors of the macro-region. Species of hard dark wood corresponding to what is called African ebony could be acquired from the north-western fringes of the Ethio-Eritrean highlands. This wood was highly appreciated for its use in the production of high-quality furniture (Espinel 2011: 125; Manzo 1999: 8). Found in roughly the same areas are also species of trees that produce aromatic resins: these resins are traditionally used in perfume production and medicine, yet arguably more important is their use for ritual purposes (Espinel 2011: 45–9, 125–6; Manzo 1999: 8). In more humid conditions, oils made of wood may have been widely produced in the Libyan desert (Moreno García 2018: 154). Finally, animal species like giraffes, felines and monkeys are present mainly in the southern sectors of the macro-region. Before the aridification process starting in the mid-Holocene these animal species were presumably more broadly distributed (Manzo 1999: 6–8). They were exploited for their skins/furs, but also were captured alive and displayed by high-ranking persons and, in the case of some species of monkeys, they were also used in ritual cultic contexts. Other very important animals in the same regions were elephants and, along the Nile, hippos, as both species were potential sources of ivory (Espinel 2011: 125; Manzo 1999: 7). Moreover, from a certain point onwards, after the Indian expedition undertaken by Alexander the Great, live elephants started being a desirable commodity. At that time African elephants were used as weapons of war, like the Indian ones, and they were also awarded an ideological,

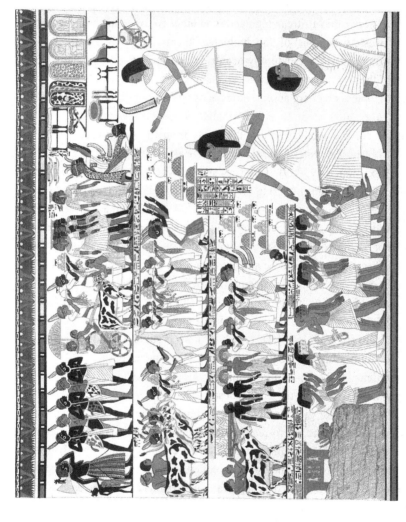

**Figure 4** The presentation of the tribute of the southern lands in the tomb of Amenhotep-Huy (TT40), dating to the reign of Tutankhamon, where several African raw materials are shown (from Lepsius 1849).

significance, especially as they were now considered symbols of universal imperial authority (Scullard 1974: 130, 199–200, 206; see Section 2.5). The occurrence in some specific sectors of the macro-region of all these highly prized commodities certainly represented an important factor in the integration and further connectivity between Egypt and its African neighbours. However, at a global scale, these commodities also increased the levels of contacts for the whole of north-eastern Africa, which was involved in even broader networks, extending from the Mediterranean to the Near East and the Indian Ocean.

In this general framework, the role of the Nile and of the Red Sea, two roughly parallel corridors crossing the tropical desert belt, cannot be over-estimated (Manzo 1999: 9–10). Water transport was certainly preferred when and where possible, because it allowed the movement of large quantities of commodities. It is important to note that a very articulated network of land routes also characterized the region. Indeed, the concentration of specific commodities in the inland areas enhanced the connections between the Nile valley and the hinterland, as did the need to bypass some areas of the Nile valley itself because of some of its topographic features, such as the cataracts, or because of specific political or economic circumstances that made transit difficult (Dumont 2009: 7; Manzo 1999: 10; see also Section 2). For this reason, although the environmental conditions in the second half of the Holocene could have transformed the regions to the east and west of the Nile valley into scarcely populated, and apparently marginal areas, they still remained crucial arteries of trade as they were crossed by routes through which commodities and raw materials could be obtained (Smith 2018: 328, 336–8). Of course, this network emerged in a setting that was already characterized by contacts and connections linking the Nile valley regions together as well as to the regions to the east and west of the river. Indeed, the pastoral economy adopted mainly by the inhabitants of the hinterland, thanks to the seasonal movements to the grazing areas and economic symbiosis with the inhabitants of the valley, resulted in enhanced contacts.

## 1.3 The Sources

The sources available to us for reconstructing the relations between Egypt and its African neighbours are both textual and archaeological, and a crucial challenge when dealing with the issue is how to combine the two (Adams 1977: 96–8). It should be stressed that the textual sources are almost exclusively from the Egyptian or external side. For example, as far as royal inscriptions are concerned – with the only notable exception of an inscription dating to the seventeenth to sixteenth centuries BC, which was made for a ruler of the kingdom of

**Figure 5** The seventeenth or early sixteenth century BC rock inscription of the
ruler of Kush 'Tr-r-h, the lion beloved of Horus lord of the desert lands' in the
Eastern Nubian Desert (courtesy Vivian Davies).

Kush (Figure 5) – the southern neighbours of Egypt did not produce written
texts until the early first millennium BC, when inscriptions by Nubian rulers
were produced (Section 2.4). Nevertheless, some Nubian royal inscriptions
dating from the third century BC to the fith century AD are poorly understood,
due to our still scarce knowledge of the Meroitic language (Rilly 2007).
Therefore, a level of bias emerges from most of the available textual evidence
that basically expresses an external view of the African neighbours of Egypt.

As far as Egyptian sources are concerned, in Antonio Loprieno's seminal
work on the subject, *Topos und Mimesis* (Loprieno 1988), he demonstrated the
ways foreigners were depicted in texts. Their iconographic representations also
changed from royal to private monuments and according to the different private
contexts. Indeed, on the one hand, some monuments produced for Africans who
were integrated into Egyptian cultural and social contexts show how mimesis
could prevail, i.e. they were presenting themselves as typical Egyptians with
few elements referring to their origin (Section 3.2). On the other hand, in the
case of monuments produced for Egyptians, the diversity of the foreigner was
emphasized and the potentially dangerous chaotic otherness it represented was
depicted as controlled by the ruler. Indeed, on royal monuments the depictions

of foreigners are precisely reduced to typified representations, also losing the individual connotations that sometimes occur on private monuments. Moreover, in general, it can be expected that written and iconographic sources are not providing complete information on the relations between Egypt and its neighbours. Indeed, they may have emphasized specific aspects and overlooked others, like for example economic exchanges if compared with over-represented military interactions, or private trade activities if compared with state-run trade.

A further feature of iconographic and textual sources is their uneven distri-bution in space and time. Some areas are very rich in this kind of evidence and this can sometimes be of some significance, such as in the case of the region of the First Cataract, which has produced a large number of documents due to its traditional role as an intermediary between Egypt and the regions to its south. But an uneven distribution of these sources can also result from specific contextual factors, such as the environment, which may or may not have favoured the preservation of written texts, such as those on perishable materials. In addition to this, the uneven distribution of documents through time may be determined by factors independent of the historical circumstances pertaining to Egyptian–African relations, as it may be due to factors related to the socio-cultural and political trajectories of the contexts in which they were produced. This may, for example, explain the larger number of texts providing data on the relations between Egypt and its neighbours dating to the Sixth Dynasty when compared to the earlier periods of the Old Kingdom. The abundance of texts for this period is likely due to the increased production of 'biographic' texts by the provincial Egyptian aristocracies following the changes to the internal balance of the Egyptian state, especially as far as the relations between the central and peripheral administration are concerned (Manzo 1999: 15).

At first glance, the archaeological evidence appears less affected by an uneven distribution across time and space and less conditioned by the ideo-logical filters affecting the texts. Nevertheless, it should be remarked also that the distribution of the archaeological remains still does not provide us with a complete picture of the past, as it too is conditioned by environmental factors that affect their preservation, and these are susceptible to variation from place to place. Moreover, some archaeological contexts are no less affected by ideo-logical factors than seen with the case of texts and iconographic representations. Exemplary are funerary contexts, whose assemblages are always highly prone to bias from ideological and religious factors, which often remain obscure to modern scholars. To cite an example from Egypt's African neighbours, the social meaning of the funerary practice of placing bucrania in graves of the Upper Nubian fifth millennium BC cemeteries may be understood as a way to

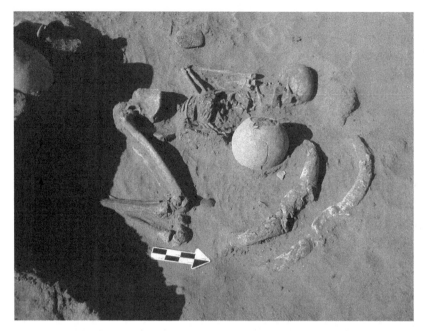

**Figure 6** A fifth millennium BC tomb with cattle skulls from cemetery R12 in Upper Nubia (© Centro Studi Sudanesi e Sub-Sahariani).

reaffirm cattle as a marker of wealth and/or status, rather than as a manifestation of a wider socio-economic strategy, as it was usually done until recent times (Figure 6; Salvatori & Usai 2019: 273–4). In the same way, it was debated whether the abundant references to cattle in the funerary assemblages of the C-Group were related to extensive cattle breeding in Lower Nubia in the late third and first half of the second millennium BC, or to the religious and socio-cultural significance of bovines, along with other animals, such as caprines, in a context of dependence, for the most part, on agriculture for subsistence (Adams 1977: 152–4).

A specific class of archaeological data affected by several limits is rock art, which occurs not only in the sectors of the Nile valley where the river crosses rocky outcrops, but also in the inland areas to the east and west of the Nile. Moreover, rock inscriptions are often associated with the rock art, that is itself regularly comprised of representations going back to different periods. Indeed, rock art sites frequently mark topographic features that functioned as landmarks for ancient peoples through the centuries (Bárta 2018: 671). For this reason, these sites often mark nodes along the main routes followed by recurrent movements, highly significant places for the study of the relations between Egypt and its African neighbours. Exemplary is the case of the Jebel Uweinat, a hilly area in the Western Desert. A scene and inscription at this site date back to the Eleventh Dynasty, most likely to the time of Mentuhotep II (Section 2.2; Figure 10). The inscription and figured scene were left by an Egyptian expedition but they are associated with rock art scenes that can be ascribed to local groups (Clayton et al. 2008). A further example is found in the Third Cataract of the Nile, where again Egyptian rock inscriptions are sometimes associated with the rock art of local groups (Osman & Edwards 2012: 257, 364). Unfortunately, the informative potential of the rock art is severely affected by the lack of precise chronology, as often only a relative date between the different representations and 'styles' characterizing each site can be established. The only way to obtain an absolute chronology is often through analysis of the similarities that can be identified between the stylistic features on the rock art and those found on well-dated monuments or objects (see e.g. Červiček 1986: 71–5). Moreover, it should also be stressed that rock art is affected by the same ideological bias characterizing both the iconographic, textual and, sometimes, the archaeological evidence. This issue should deter us from considering rock art representations as faithful evidence of the history of the region they are located in. For example, representations of boats found at a site located in what is today an area of desert, cannot be certainly linked to the remote humid phases when the rivers crossing the deserts were flowing or necessarily act as a reference to real navigations on the Nile or the Red Sea. Such scenes could instead be explained by the ideological and religious meanings ascribed to boats in Egypt which were perhaps also shared by the cultures of its neighbour regions.

## 2 Egypt and Its African Neighbours

### 2.1 Livestock, Crops and Exotica

With the change of the climatic setting taking place from around the end of the seventh millennium BC (Section 1.2), the groups inhabiting both the Nile valley and the inland areas were forced to experiment and find new solutions for the new climate. This process ultimately led to the adoption of subsistence systems based on the exploitation of domesticated animals and plants. This probably took place in the framework of contacts with the Near East, another area that also faced similar environmental challenges (Salvatori & Usai 2019: 257–8).

With particular regard to the Egyptian case, the groups living east and west of the Nile valley may have been crucial in this process (Riemer & Kindermann 2019: 210–12). It may sound somehow strange that the regions beyond the river valley may have played a crucial role in these social and economic changes, as we are used to thinking of river valleys as the 'cradles of civilizations'. Nevertheless, it is evident that, even when environmental conditions started changing, the Nile continued flowing and the availability of resources did not change that much in the valley, even when there were perhaps lower water levels in the river. On the contrary, in areas beyond the valley, even small variations in water availability could have more important consequences. This may explain why the earliest evidence of the adoption of domesticated plants and animals was found not in the valley, but in areas and sites that lie away from the river itself (Wengrow et al. 2014: 97–8). A good example of this situation is represented by the Fayum region, where traces of cereal cultivation date back to the fifth millennium BC (Wendrich et al. 2010). Indeed, the Fayum is itself strictly speaking outside of the Nile valley, and there cultivation may have been conducted in areas far from the shores of Nile-fed Lake Qarun (Wengrow et al. 2014: 97–8). In the Nile valley south of Egypt, the role of agriculture has largely been overlooked until very recent times due to a lack of data. However, agriculture may have been relevant there too, especially when considering the recently recorded evidence of exploitation of Near Eastern domesticated crops at the end of the sixth millennium BC in Upper Nubia (Salvatori & Usai 2019: 259–61). As roughly contemporary evidence of Near Eastern crops was found in the Fayum, in the Delta, but not in the Egyptian Nile valley proper, it can therefore be suggested that domesticated plants were reaching the riverine regions to the south of Egypt via the groups living on the fringes of the valley, although the precise trajectories they took remain debated due to the limited available evidence. Further south, the earliest evidence of domestication of Sahelian crops was also recorded, far from the Nile valley, in Eastern Sudan, and dates to the fourth millennium BC (Winchell et al. 2017).

A further example of the crucial role played by inland areas in the introduction of the new adaptive strategies is the site of Sodmein cave, in the Egyptian Eastern Desert. There, the earliest evidence of domesticated caprines, certainly arriving from the Near East, was found in the assemblages dating to the very end of the seventh millennium BC (Vermeersch et al. 2015). As far as the domesticated cattle are concerned, the earliest verifiable occurrence in the Western Desert is from Nabta Playa and dates to the sixth millennium BC (Brass 2018: 107–8). The earliest evidence of domesticated bovines in the Nile valley is not from Egypt, but was found in Upper Nubia, in assemblages dating to the first half of the sixth millennium BC. Although an African domestication of wild bovines was proposed in the past, it has now been confirmed that domesticated cattle were arriving from the Near East (Brass 2018: 103–4; Salvatori & Usai 2019: 256–7). It can therefore be suggested that domesticated cattle and caprines were also reaching the Nile valley via the groups living on its fringes or in inland regions. Indeed, as was the case for domesticated crops, the precise trajectories they took remain to be clarified.

Be that as it may, it is evident that in this phase the relations between the Egyptian Nile valley and its African neighbours, in particular the inland areas, were certainly very important. Indeed, this network of relations, through which the domesticated species arrived in the Egyptian Nile valley, was perhaps already in existence in earlier times due to the environmental diversity and economic interdependence between the valley and its hinterland (Section 1.2), and can be perhaps traced in the material culture (Riemer & Kindermann 2019: 203; and see the end of this section). In general, if the whole of north-eastern Africa is considered, some groups from the inland regions may have intensified their frequentation of the river valleys and the areas with greater water availability, such as the fringes of the Ethio-Eritrean highlands, on a seasonal basis, with yearly repeated displacements in the dry season, in a phase increasingly affected by the environmental and climatic changes. In the meantime, some groups also started migrating towards regions with better environmental conditions (Gatto & Zerboni 2015: 318, 322). The Nile valley was certainly one of those regions (Gatto 2011; Smith 2018: 327–8). Its dynamic interactions with the inner areas may not only have contributed to the spread of some of the innovations in the field of the subsistence economy, but also to the emergence of other aspects of Egyptian culture in terms of ideology and religion (Darnell 2007: 30–1; see also Section 3.3). It should be stressed that climatic change was a gradual and progressive process, taking place in the northern regions earlier than in the rest of north-eastern Africa (Section 1.2). In the northern regions it was almost completed at the end of the third millennium BC, and only occurred later in the southern regions, where more humid conditions continued up until the very end of the second millennium BC. Therefore, such intensified contacts with the inland areas did not affect the whole Nile basin at the same time. They intensified at different moments according to the changes in the local environmental conditions and continued to be a crucial factor in the processes of interaction between the regions in the phases that followed as well.

Indeed, as far as the Lower Nile valley is concerned, archaeological traces of the interactions with its hinterland are well evident in the material culture. Lithic technologies, such as the bifacial pressure flake technique, apparently spread from the Western Desert to the Predynastic cultures at an early stage (Kuper 2002: 5–9). Later on, in the second half of the Holocene, the occurrence of sites featuring Predynastic-related material culture in the regions to the east and west of the Nile valley suggests that interactions between the inland regions and the valley were continuing (see, e.g., Friedman & Hobbs 2002: 188–9; Wengrow et al. 2014: 107). These interactions were perhaps favoured by the economic interdependence between the two areas, as well as perhaps by seasonal and/or permanent movements of the human groups. A further element showing the interaction between the Egyptian Nile valley and its hinterland in this phase is certainly represented by the similarities found in the Predynastic iconographies and the rock art occurring in the regions east and west of the Nile valley. These similarities strongly suggest contacts between the inhabitants of the two areas and/or the possibility that the same groups may have frequented the two areas. Indeed, with some of the iconographies occurring in the Predynastic art and in the rock art being perhaps related to ideas that were crucial elements in later Egyptian ideology and religion, this fact may also lead to the hypothesis that some of these concepts may have been elaborated not in the Nile valley, but in its hinterland (Section 3.3).

Noteworthy in this phase is not only the fact that the ties between valley and its hinterland were very strong, but that so were those held between the different sectors of the Nile valley. This becomes very evident when the ceramic traditions of these regions are considered. Indeed, until late Naqada II times, the Upper Egyptian ceramic tradition is characterized by several elements that also occur in the upstream sectors of the Nile valley, such as the black-topped pottery, the rippled ware and the so-called Tasian beakers (Smith 2018: 331). Moreover, objects related to body decoration, such as personal ornaments, tools used for the preparation of cosmetics and some elements of the funeral rituals appear to have a wide distribution in sites of the whole Nile valley across the fifth millennium BC (Wengrow et al. 2014: 104–7). Among the shared traits in the material culture of several regions of the Nile valley in this phase were also the mace-heads. These typically occur in the funerary assemblages and represent a kind of weapon, which was also very prominently used as a marker of rank. This view is supported by the fact that in several contexts in the Nile valley mace-heads are associated with the richer graves that can be ascribed to more influential individuals. Noteworthy also is the use of this kind of archaic weapon in dynastic Egypt by the ruler when fighting his enemies, representing the chaotic forces. From the earliest to the latest iconographic documents of Egyptian kingship, these weapons maintained a crucial ideological meaning, although from a certain point onwards they were no longer likely to have been used in real battles.

Indeed, starting from the fifth millennium BC, evidence of the emergence of social hierarchies occurs in several regions of the Nile valley, from Egypt to the area of the confluence between Blue and White Nile. This may have favoured an increasing interest in exotic commodities that were used to produce prestige objects to be displayed as rank markers. Moreover, both in Egypt and upstream regions, objects made from rare and exotic raw materials may have been used in gift-giving exchanges between elites. The exchange of such objects aimed at maintaining the elite social relations and networks, which was also a well-known practice in later phases (see, e.g., Morkot 2013: 922). Furthermore, this may have made the availability of such commodities a crucial factor in the stability of the power of the elites. Returning to the mace-heads, they were made from very hard stones available in the inland regions. In the case of the example found in a tomb in the Lower Nubian Cemetery 137 at Sayala (Firth 1927: 204–10), which can be ascribed to a member of the local A-Group elite, the handle of the mace was covered with gold sheet (Figure 7). This gold sheet was also made from a raw material that was most likely obtained from inland regions to the east of the Nile valley.

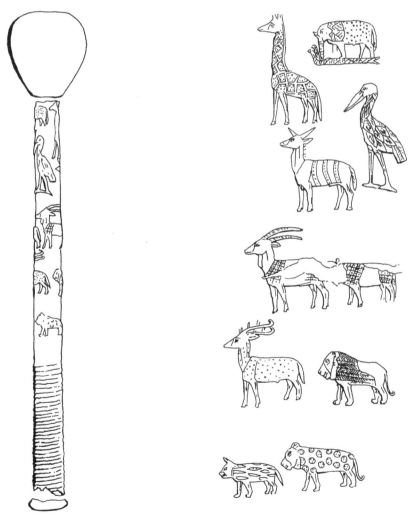

**Figure 7** A mace from an A-Group elite tomb in Cemetery 137 at Sayala in Lower Nubia (from Firth 1927).

The desire for rare raw materials and commodities certainly enhanced the pre-existing networks of relations and exchanges involving Egypt and its African neighbours. Indeed, it was the rise of the Egyptian state at the end of the fourth millennium BC that further increased the demand for exotic raw materials (Trigger 1987). The objects made from prized raw materials from the southern regions played a key role in the maintenance and reproduction of social relations inside the fledging Egyptian state. Furthermore, this represented a powerful stimulus in what became a greater involvement of the Egyptian state in the regions south of the First Cataract, as well as in the regions east and west of the river valley, where some raw materials were available or which were crossed by important trade routes (Section 1.2.). It is noteworthy that these kinds of dynamics never came to an end in the following phases of the interactions between Egypt and its African neighbours and show signs of continuation over long periods of time.

## 2.2 Competing Powers, Alternative Routes

In attempting to obtain exotic and prized commodities, the Egyptian elite had to deal with the groups controlling the regions that the commodities themselves flowed through. As noted in Section 2.1, dominant social hierarchies also emerged in many of those regions, with an increased demand of their own for prized commodities to be used as rank markers. This is very evident in the case of Lower Nubia, the sector of the Nile valley between the First and the Second Cataract (i.e. immediately south of the fledging Egyptian state), where an archaeological culture named A-Group dated between 3800 and 2900 BC is found (Gatto 2006). At least in the later phases of its development, the A-Group certainly saw the emergence of a complex social structure. This is evident in the A-Group funerary contexts, such as the aforementioned tomb in Cemetery 137 at Sayala, but is especially the case in the exceptional tombs in the L Cemetery at Qustul, immediately to the north of the Second Cataract. There, several tombs notable for their exceptional size and grave goods have been discovered (Gatto 2006: 70–2).

The A-Group elite was certainly involved in the exchange of commodities with Egypt, as suggested by the presence of Egyptian imports concentrated in the main A-Group centres where the elite resided (Takamiya 2004: 52–5, 57–8). The clear ability of the A-Group elite to manage the flow of commodities from the more southern regions, and to obtain Egyptian goods in exchange, was of course due to the fact that it strategically controlled the sector of the Nile valley immediately south of the First Cataract, through which most of these commodities could reach Egypt. In addition, the A-Group may have featured a pastoral mobile component, which visited the hinterland east and west of the Lower Nubian Nile valley at least on a seasonal basis. This mobile part of the population may have enhanced the possibility of also getting raw materials from inland regions (Gatto 2006: 71). It should also be stressed that the groups inhabiting the inland areas may have played an important role in this dynamic trade. However, this unfortunately remains largely obscure due to the scarce archaeological exploration of the desert regions. Yet the role of the local groups was suggested for the Wadi Allaqi area, one of the main gold-bearing regions of the Eastern Desert. In this region, gold objects have been found and the evidence of gold exploitation can be ascribed to local groups dating to the fifth millennium BC (Sadr 1997: 68–73) (Figure 8).

From a certain point onwards, the control over the trade of most of the African commodities by the A-Group elite may have forced the Egyptian state to avoid this middleman and gain a more direct access to the flow of goods. This may have caused an increasing political and military pressure on Lower Nubia, which ultimately resulted in the end of the A-Group culture and the adoption of a more mobile style of life by the groups inhabiting the region (Török 2009: 49–54). The attempts by the Egyptian state to control the exchange network also resulted in the establishment of an outpost in Nubia at

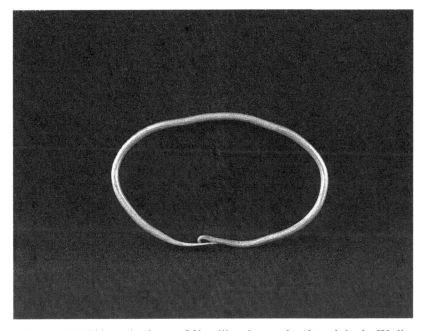

**Figure 8** Gold bracelet from a fifth millennium BC local tomb in the Wadi Allaqi (Photographer Rocco Ricci © The British Museum).

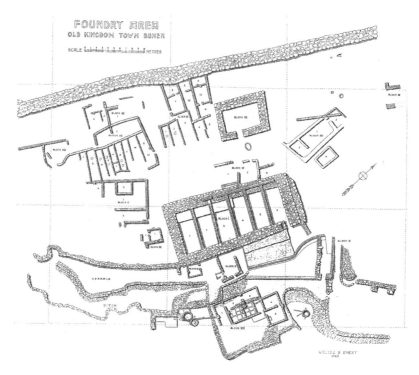

**Figure 9** Map of a sector of the Old Kingdom Egyptian outpost
at Buhen (from *Kush* 11, courtesy National Corporation for Antiquities and Museums).

Buhen (Figure 9), on the northern end of the Second Cataract, and perhaps
a second one at Kubban, at the entrance of the Wadi Allaqi, a crucial route to
reach the gold mines of the Eastern Nubian Desert (O'Connor 2014: 327–8).
These settlements were certainly strategically placed to ensure that Egypt was
supplied with the much wanted African commodities during the Fourth Dynasty
and had connections with the Egyptian administration. In the case of Buhen,
these connections are demonstrated by the seal impressions, which often mention royal names. Interestingly, some recently published sealings from Buhen
may also suggest – at least for that site – an earlier phase of occupation, dating to
the First and perhaps even the Second Dynasty (Torcia 2020: 27–46).
Apparently, this new model of interaction imposed by the expanding Egyptian
state worked efficiently for several centuries. Actually, the latest royal names on
the Buhen sealings are those of late Fifth Dynasty rulers. After the Fifth
Dynasty, Buhen was abandoned perhaps in the wake of socio-political changes
to the area. That changes occurred in Lower Nubia finds confirmation in the
presence of new Nubian centres in the region, which are attested by cemeteries
and settlements pertaining to the C-Group culture. This culture perhaps

originated ca. 2500 BC from groups previously living in the deserts pushed to move more permanently into Lower Nubia by the increasing aridity and/or from movement north of groups from upstream regions (Török 2009: 53–4, 62–3).

To understand the dynamics related to the abandonment of the Egyptian outpost(s) in Lower Nubia, it may be interesting to highlight that we have increasing textual evidence of Egyptian interest in navigation of the Red Sea roughly dating to the same period (Espinel 2011: 186–92, 198–200; Manzo 1999: 16–19). Indeed, in the Fifth and in the Sixth Dynasties, Egyptian navigation of the Red Sea was not only aimed at getting access to the mining regions of Sinai, as it was certainly in the Fourth Dynasty, but also to reach the regions in the southern Red Sea, where the same African commodities that were arriving in Egypt also via Nubia could be obtained. In particular, these maritime expeditions were reaching a land named Punt, whose location was for a long time debated but can now be confidently placed in a vast region extending from Eastern Sudan to the Eritrean coast and perhaps, at least from Twelfth Dynasty times, also to the opposite Arabian coast (Espinel 2011: 273; see also Breyer 2016). Interestingly, during the Sixth Dynasty and perhaps even a bit earlier, the Egyptian state also systematically extended its influence into the Western Desert: an important administrative centre was established in the oasis of Dakhla, several watching points were placed along the perimeter of the same oasis (Kaper & Willems 2002), and a system of watering and stopping points was established along the routes departing from the oasis and leading to the south and south-west (Förster 2013: 299–306). Some texts going back to the same phases also mention Egyptian activities along the tracks of the Western Desert, through which the regions where African commodities were available could also be reached. Therefore, perhaps the arrival in Lower Nubia of new groups was compromising the control over the Nile routes and this led to the attempt to bypass it both on the western and eastern side, respectively via the Western Desert and via the Red Sea. Nevertheless, in the light of some passages in Egyptian texts of this phase and considering that the site of Buhen does not show any evidence of destruction, it cannot be excluded that some kind of impediment in the flow of commodities occurred even further south in the Nile valley.

The most famous and important text describing the interaction between the Egyptians and their southern neighbours in this specific phase is certainly the 'biography' of nobleman Harkhuf. Harkhuf belonged to a family administering the southernmost Egyptian *nome*, the first of Upper Egypt, centred in Elephantine and therefore in charge of controlling the southern border for the ruler (Obsomer 2007: 41–3). The 'biographic' inscription was carved on the façade of his rock-cut tomb at Qubbet el-Hawa, not far from Aswan. It states that Harkhuf conducted two expeditions during the reign of Merenra and one during the reign of Pepy II, at the end of the Sixth Dynasty. While the description of the first expedition is very short, the description of the second specifies that the 'route of Elephantine' was followed. In the third expedition, the 'route of the Oasis' was used by Harkhuf. The final destination of the expeditions was the land of Yam, where, according to the inscription, ebony, incense, other aromatics and oils, leopard skins, ivory tusks and throwing sticks could be obtained. A further interesting element in the inscription of Harkhuf emerges from the letter of King Pepy II copied at the end of the 'biographic' text: the king congratulates Harkhuf on his return from the last trip because he was able to bring with him a 'pigmy' (or dwarf?) to perform the sacred dances, as the treasurer Bawrdjed had earlier done during the time of King Isesi (Obsomer 2007: 43). Indeed, this mention of a pigmy, together with the escort of recruits from Yam accompanying Harkhuf on his way back, shows a further commodity that could be obtained from the southern regions by the Egyptian state: labour. Of course, this was not the first nor the last time that individuals or groups of people from inland and upstream regions arrived in Egypt. Other textual and iconographic documents suggest that such mobility was fairly common (Section 3.2). Indeed, recruits from Nubian and Libyan regions were already mentioned in the inscription of Weni, which reported the deeds completed during the reign of Pepy I. At that time, the recruits were incorporated into the Egyptian army for a campaign conducted in the Palestinian area (Piacentini 1990: 16–17).

In the third journey, it is specified that, while on the 'route of the Oasis', the caravan led by Harkhuf met the ruler of Yam on his way to fight the Temehu (i.e. the Libyans – see Moreno García 2018: 153). This is certainly a very intriguing statement, as the location of Yam is still debated and different hypotheses have been proposed (Obsomer 2007: 43–50). Although a location along the Nile, in Upper Nubia or near the confluence of the Atbara into the Nile, was up until recently the preferred choice for most scholars, the discovery of a hieroglyphic rock inscription mentioning Yam likely to date to the time of Mentuhotep II has challenged this theory (Figure 10). This inscription is in the Jebel Uweinat, which is more than 500 km west of the Nile valley, and this may suggest a more remote location for Yam in the south-west of Egypt (Cooper 2012: 17–21; Förster 2013: 319–20).

From the description of Harkhuf's expeditions, the diplomatic and perhaps military aspects of the activities he conducted during his trips also emerge. Indeed, several passages mention the Nubian rulers with whom he was interacting, along with the trade exchanges and diplomatic-political relations converging upon the networks of Egypt and its African neighbours. It seems that while

**Figure 10** Rock inscription of the Eleventh Dynasty at Jebel Uweinat, most likely dating to the time of King Mentuhotep II (courtesy Laure Pantalacci).

Harkhuf had to deal with a ruler of Satjw and Irtjet during the second expedition, in the third there was only one person ruling over Satjw, Irtjet and Wawat (Obsomer 2007: 41–2). This fact, together with the need for an escort to cross the territory under the control of this ruler, suggests a certain instability in the political setting of the Nubian Nile valley.

Therefore, one side of the Harkhuf inscription confirms the Egyptian state's continuous interest in acquiring highly sought-after African commodities. The other side shows the very complex political and social setting of the regions south of Egypt, due to the rise and development of complex organizations and politics in the Middle Nile regions. Indeed, we know that social hierarchies also emerged south of the Lower Nubia, at least from the fifth millennium BC onwards (Honegger 2014: 41). This is clearly demonstrated by the funerary evidence, yet other data exist to confirm these social changes: some storage pits for cereals dating to the first half of the third millennium BC were found on the island of Sai. These were associated with sealings, which demonstrate that some administration of these stores was taking place (Anderson & Welsby 2004: 69). Further south, near Kerma, a large and well-organized settlement surrounded by earth bastions suggests that a complex and highly organized community inhabited the region in the early third millennium BC (Honegger 2014: 111). As the Harkhuf inscription described, ca. 2200 BC the southern polities were apparently progressively unifying and sometimes fighting with each other. These tensions were evidently the result of much earlier dynamics, and these could now threaten the Egyptian activities in those regions. In this general context, Upper Nubia and Lower Nubia came under the control of several powerful and sometimes hostile polities. It is evident that the earlier Egyptian outposts between the First and the Second Cataract were no longer useful for obtaining direct access to the African commodities and perhaps from a certain point onwards they could have become even unsafe. This may have led to their abandonment at the end of the Fifth Dynasty. At that point, African commodities could only then be obtained by conducting direct maritime and/or land expeditions, bypassing the political instability surrounding Nubia and any middlemen.

With the end of the Sixth Dynasty and the loss of the internal cohesion of the Egyptian state, the number of textual and iconographic sources documenting interactions between Egypt and its African neighbours decreases. Nevertheless, it is debatable whether this decrease was related to a lesser intensity in interaction or whether it was the types and ways the interaction took place that changed. Indeed, the weakening of the Egyptian state may have led to the end of the large-scale land and maritime expeditions, such as those described at the end of the Old Kingdom. However, we cannot exclude the possibility that smaller-scale interactions intensified, which left more room for individual initiatives on the Egyptian side, while the Nubian involvement in the management of interactions and exchanges may have in the meantime increased. Certainly, this new situation did not lead to a decreased Nubian presence in Egypt (Section 3.2).

Be that as it may, at the beginning of the Middle Kingdom, the general pattern of the interaction between Egypt and its African neighbours was not that different from the one marking the end of the Old Kingdom. The aforementioned inscription likely to date to the time of Mentuhotep II at Jebel Uweinat

(Figure 10), and an inscription of the time of Mentuhotep III in the Wadi Hammamat, which mentions an expedition to the land of Punt (Lichtheim 1988: 52–4), both point to a possible resumption of the expedition strategy of the earlier period. The strategy was focussed on large-scale expeditions that crossed both the Western and Eastern Desert and the Red Sea in order to access the African commodities. In the valley to the south of Egypt, some initiatives of the Eleventh Dynasty rulers may have resulted in the restoration of a certain influence over Lower Nubia, perhaps also thanks to alliances established with the local rulers, which may have been crucial also in the reunification of Egypt, as suggested by the stela or Idudju-Iker (Wegner 2017–2018, 184–94). Despite this, we have no mention of trade expeditions following the Nile, as was the case at the end of the Old Kingdom. This lacuna of trade along the Nile may be due to the political evolution of the regions south of the Second Cataract, where a highly structured Nubian polity emerged. This is mentioned for the first time in an inscription found in the fortress of Buhen, a newly established cornerstone of the Egyptian presence in Nubia, not far from the Old Kingdom outpost mentioned before (Emery et al. 1979). The inscription refers to Mentuhotep, a commander of the army during the reign of Senwsert I, at the beginning of the Twelfth Dynasty, who led a military campaign against a Nubian alliance. Amongst the polities/regions joining the alliance was Kush, which was perhaps even a crucial partner in it if its position at the top of the list of partners in the campaign can be taken to indicate the order of importance (Obsomer 2007: 60–1). From this moment onwards, Kush was the name used to label a polity that, at the peak of its power, controlled Upper Nubia and extended its influence over the regions around it. Its main administrative and ceremonial centre was located at Kerma, south of the Third Cataract, a settlement with huge, monumental structures, temples and palaces character-ized by a distinct architectural style, and a neatly laid-out urban structure (Figure 11) (Bonnet 2014). In the cemetery nearby, the earliest of many large-scale monumental tombs marked by tumulus was identified as a royal tomb, dating to the very end of the third millennium BC (Honegger 2018).

Therefore, the end of the Egyptian expeditions along the Nile may have been due to the rise of a Nubian state controlling the flow of commodities along the river. The fact that south of the border the control of trade was in the hands of the Nubians is evident in some Egyptian texts, such as the one inscribed on a border stela of Senwsert III found in the fortress of Semna, on the Second Cataract: in association with the usual description of the defeat of the Nubians by the king and the commitment to push them back at the frontier, there is an explicit mention of Nubian traders being indeed allowed to cross the border and to go to the fortress of Iken (Mirgissa) for trading purposes (Obsomer 2007: 66, 70).

**Figure 11** Map of the city of Kerma in Upper Nubia at the end of its development, ca. 1500 BC (© Mission Suisse-Franco-Soudanaise de Kerma/ Doukki Gel).

The Semna dispatches, messages sent by the commanders of the fortress controlling the southern border of Egypt to update the central administration on the border situation at the time of Amenemhat III, mention how groups of foreigners trying to enter Lower Nubia were repelled. Again, the arrival of Nubian traders, who were authorized to pass the border, is mentioned (Smither 1945: 6, 10). Archaeologically, the active involvement of the Nubian rulers in those long-distance exchanges is supported not only by the Egyptian imports occurring in contexts related to the Kerma elite, but also by the large storage facilities near the palaces and the temples in the capital of Kush, which were sometimes certainly used for precious commodities (Bonnet 2004: 115, 2014: 209–11).

Military campaigns south of Lower Nubia were undertaken by the Egyptian rulers from the early Twelfth Dynasty up until the time of Senwsert III (Obsomer 2007: 58–69). This policy can be interpreted as an attempt to gain direct control of the African commodities flowing along the river. But all these attempts failed: the limit of Egyptian control remained at the southern end of the Second Cataract. A chain of imposing fortresses was built to control Lower Nubia and to protect the southern border, as perhaps the kingdom of Kush remained a threat to Egypt, who in the meantime managed to control the exchanges with Nubian traders. Indeed, Nubian traders, the caravans and the boats loaded with the African commodities were not only allowed to pass but perhaps also supported in passing through the Second Cataract, one of the more difficult parts of the Nile to navigate (Vogel 2010: 10–12). In this general framework, the continuation and perhaps even intensification of the Egyptian activities in the Red Sea during the Middle Kingdom can be interpreted as a systematic attempt to gain greater access to the production areas of those commodities by bypassing the middleman of Kerma in the valley. Similar attempts at bypassing areas of the Nile valley via the network of land routes crossing the Western Desert are recorded up until the Eleventh Dynasty (see the beginning of this Section), but these were later abandoned, perhaps also because of the progressive extension of the arid conditions, which may have affected the efficiency of the land routes (Section 1.2).

The interactions between Egypt and the regions of north-eastern Africa via the Red Sea are known to have taken place for this phase thanks to the archaeological investigations of the harbour at Mersa/Wadi Gawasis and the textual evidence collected therein (Bard & Fattovich 2018). In particular, these investigations throw light on the complex organization of the Egyptian expeditions: the boats, largely made from cedar wood imported from Byblos (on the coast of modern Lebanon), were built in Coptos on the Nile, and then dismantled and reassembled on the Red Sea coast (Figure 12). A complex system provided the expeditions with all the supplies they needed, while the routes linking the harbour to the Nile valley were kept safe. The involvement of Nubians, and perhaps also Levantines, as qualified labour in these expeditions is suggested by archaeological finds. Moreover, imported materials indicate that the southern Red Sea regions were involved in the exchange network forged through the Egyptian expeditions. This

**Figure 12** A cedar plank from boat building and some cargo boxes in a late Twelfth Dynasty assemblage at Mersa/Wadi Gawasis (© 'L'Orientale', ISMEO and Boston University Joint Expedition at Mersa/Wadi Gawasis).

network extended from the Nubian Eastern Desert to Eastern Sudan and the Eritrean coast and also included the southern coastal strip of the Arabian peninsula. Therefore, the region named Punt by the Egyptians may, at least in this phase, correspond to a very broad area, even if it is likely the Egyptian expeditions were only accessing some specific points of it (Manzo 2010: 448–9).

## 2.3 Between Exploitation and Entanglement

The loose cohesion of the Egyptian state at the end of the Middle Kingdom certainly led to an increasing Nubian influence in the management of the exchanges between Egypt and upstream regions. Indeed, some texts throw light on the expansion of the kingdom of Kush. One of these texts is an inscription recorded in the tomb of Sebeknakht, a local governor of El Kab, in Upper Egypt, and mentions a raid in the region conducted by an alliance led by Kush and also involving Wawat (certainly Lower Nubia), Khent-en-Nefer (a region of Upper Nubia), Medja (most likely the Eastern Desert) and Punt (for which see Section 2.2) (Davies 2003) (Figure 13). This text demonstrates the extension of the political influence of Kush into the neighbouring regions. A second important text is a well-known stele of the Theban ruler Kamose. Part of this stele describes the capture of the envoy of the Hyksos ruler, who controlled Lower Egypt, to the king of Kush by the Theban forces on the 'route of the Oasis' (Smith & Smith 1976: 61). This passage demonstrates on one hand the alliance between Hyksos and Kush, which was threatening the Theban polity, while on the other the ability of Kush to extend its network of political and presumably also economic relations towards the Mediterranean and the Near East.

The data emerging from these two texts are supported by the archaeological evidence, with the imposing monumental structures in the city of Kerma (Figure 1), as well as the funerary chapels in the cemetery reaching imposing dimensions, being particularly exemplary (Bonnet 2000; 2004). Indeed, the royal tumuli in the cemetery are of unprecedented dimensions and complexity, also in terms of the grave goods they contain, and they usually include a large number of sacrificed individuals (Reisner 1923a: 135–473). Moreover, in Lower Nubia, archaeological and epigraphic traces suggest the intensification of interactions with Upper Nubia (i.e. with the core area of the kingdom of Kush). In this phase the Lower Nubian Egyptian fortresses established during the Middle Kingdom were under the political control of the king of Kush, as shown by several inscriptions (Török 2009: 103–17). In the meantime, in both the Western (Jesse et al. 2004) and Eastern Deserts, as well as in Eastern Sudan (Manzo 2012: 77, 81), material traces of contact with the Kerma culture of Upper Nubia are visible. A so far unique hieroglyphic inscription of a king of Kush was also recorded in the Eastern Desert, which suggests the extension of the kingdom's sphere of influence into the area (Davies 2014: 35–6) (Figure 5). The fact that this powerful Upper Nubian state may have established a broad system of alliances in north-eastern Africa is perhaps also shown by the number and variety of types of sanctuaries and structures brought to light in its main administrative and ceremonial centre at Kerma (Bonnet 2004: 113, 139).

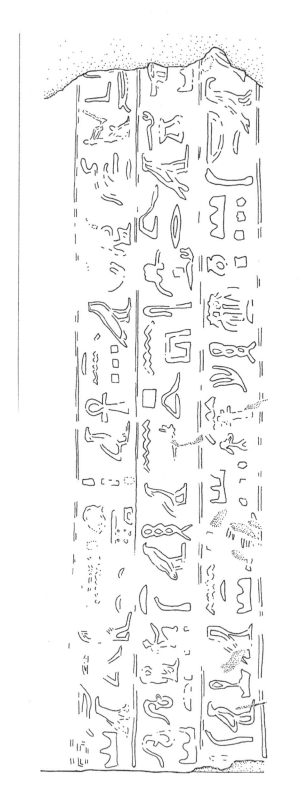

**Figure 13** Inscription in the tomb of Sebeknakht at El Kab mentioning a Kushite raid in Upper Egypt in the Second Intermediate Period (courtesy Vivian Davies).

The Theban rulers of the Seventeenth and early Eighteenth Dynasty faced at the same time the Nubian and the Hyksos threat, and this led first to the restoration of Egyptian control over Lower Nubia, and after that to several expeditions south of the Second Cataract. It was Thutmosis I who conducted an in-depth campaign (Török 2009: 157–61), most likely ravaging Kerma itself and reaching the southernmost point ever reached by Egyptian political control in Africa. The upstream frontier was established at Hagar el-Merwa, between the Fourth and the Fifth Cataracts (Davies 2017; Section 3.3; Figures 29–31). Thutmosis I also built a temple and established a fortified settlement at Dukki Gel, not far from Kerma (Bonnet 2008: 75). This site is of much interest due to its architectural history. Stratigraphic studies demonstrate how fragile Egyptian control over the region was at the beginning of the Eighteenth Dynasty, and how determined and fierce Nubian opposition was against the occupation. Indeed, the earlier Egyptian settlement was destroyed and apparently abandoned and there is evidence of occupation levels with Nubian materials overlapping its remains. This is also reflected in contemporary texts, such as a rock inscription of Thutmosis II near Aswan that mentions a military campaign in response to an uprising in Nubia also involving the royal family of Kush (Gabolde 2003: 133). It was only after the further military actions of Thutmosis III that full control was established over the region (Török 2009: 162–4). At that time, the boundary inscriptions at Hagar el-Merwa were renewed (Davies 2017). Noteworthy during this period of instability in Upper Nubia is the organization of a maritime expedition to the land of Punt. Indeed, this event is one of the most famous moments in relations between Egypt and the southern regions: Queen Hatshepsut organized an expedition to Punt, extensively recorded by texts and representations in her temple at Deir el-Bahari (Espinel 2011: 327–75). Similar to the previous ones (Section 2.2), the expedition aimed at gaining greater access to African materials. At first sight, when there was a possibility of obtaining such goods via trade coming through Upper Nubia, as after the conquest of the region by Thutmosis I, such a complex enterprise remains unexplained. Indeed, this expedition was most likely organized for the reason that control over Upper Nubia had been temporarily halted by the aforementioned Nubian riots.

This also confirms that the aim of Egyptian expansion into Upper Nubia in this period was not only related to the need to neutralize a southern menace, that, as stressed earlier, was threatening Egypt, but also to gain direct access to the sources of the African raw materials. This is very evident in the case of gold, with an increasing direct Egyptian involvement in the exploitation of the gold sources in the Nubian Eastern Desert. This is clearly demonstrated by textual and iconographic evidence (Morkot 2013: 938–9), as well as by rock inscriptions and archaeological remains recorded in the gold-bearing areas (Davies 2014: 41–2). Therefore, the newly established Egyptian cities in Nubia, whose central space usually consisted of a temple surrounded by huge storage facilities (Kemp 1972), should not only be interpreted as administrative centres aimed at controlling and exploiting the newly conquered areas, but also as nodes of a network of economic and political relations extending well beyond the regions under the Egyptian administration. Interactions with African regions, such as those in the Eastern Desert and Irem, a region whose name is frequently mentioned in the New Kingdom texts (see O'Connor 1987), were certainly not limited to the military confrontation emphasized in the texts, but also included exchange and trade. Although archaeological investigation of the trade in African commodities may be difficult because of the perishable (or, in the case of gold and other metals, reusable) nature of those materials, some texts, such as the Annals of Thutmosis III in the temple of Karnak, and artistic representations, such as the scenes of Nubian tribute in the private tombs of officials, are very informative (Panagiotopoulos 2006). The Annals of Thutmosis III list huge amounts of goods arriving from different territories: not only are crops, cattle and labour arriving from the Nubian Nile valley listed, but also gold, most likely extracted from the Eastern Desert, people and raw materials ultimately originating from areas outside direct Egyptian control. This was perhaps the case of Irem and this was certainly the case with Punt, which is also mentioned in the Annals. The clearest iconographic attestation of the arrival of the tribute from the southern lands is certainly the one represented in the Theban tomb of Amenhotep nick-named Huy, who acted as 'royal son of Kush' (i.e. governor of Nubia), during the reign of Tutankhamon (Davies & Gardiner 1926: pl. 26; Figure 4). In this depiction not only are the different raw materials depicted, but also the finished objects that were likely to have been produced in Nubia. Alongside these were wild animals and cattle, as well as prisoners and foreign princesses. The representation of members of the Nubian elite in a scene of Nubian tribute shows once again the close relationship between the economic exchanges and the diplomatic and political ties between Egypt and its African neighbours. Indeed, in this phase it was a well-known practice to have the young members of Nubian aristocratic families educated in Egypt. Although they were technically hostages and their presence in Egypt ensured the good conduct of their relatives in their homeland, at the same time they were absorbing Egyptian culture and establishing personal ties with members of the Egyptian elite (Morkot 2013: 945–50; see also Section 3.2). When the boys became adults, some of them returned home as state officials to administer the Egyptian Nubian dominions. In the meantime, the female members of the Nubian elite families could join the royal harem, as perhaps suggested by the scene in the tomb of Huy.

As we will see, if these kinds of practices favoured the adoption of Egyptian culture by the Nubian aristocracies, which posed long-term consequences, in this way some traits of Nubian culture could also spread among the Egyptian elite (Section 3.3). Of course, cultural entanglement also took place in Nubia itself: the presence of Nubians in the newly established Egyptian administrative centres is well evident in both the settlements and the cemeteries, and a new and original culture emerged from this process of interaction and reciprocal influence. Evidence of this new culture is suggested by the female burials recorded in the cemetery at Tombos, not far from the Third Cataract, where an Egyptian administrative centre was established in the early Eighteenth Dynasty. Nubian women most likely played a crucial role in this settlement, as they became important members of the community and the presence of mixed couples is also highly possible (Smith 2003: 162–6, 205). The women interred in the cemeteries at Tombos were buried according to Nubian funerary traditions, while the presence of Nubian cooking vessels suggests that they also brought their cuisine with them: perhaps new foodways combining Egyptian and Nubian elements were emerging in those contexts.

The Egyptian administrative centres upstream of Tombos, which were identified on archaeological or textual basis, are few in number: the aforementioned Egyptian town at Dukki Gel, rebuilt after the destructive Nubian riots in the early Eighteenth Dynasty, the site of Kawa, which was most likely established in Amarnian times, as suggested by its Egyptian name 'Finding the Aten', and Napata, in the area of Jebel Barkal, where an important centre was also established in the Eighteenth Dynasty. This situation contrasts with the concentration of Egyptian centres in the region downstream of the Third Cataract. This uneven distribution of Egyptian centres in Nubia pointed to a different kind of control being exercised in the northern part of the region closer to Egypt, with more direct control by the Egyptian administration, while in the southern part of Nubia perhaps a less direct method of control was put in place, thanks to a wider involvement of the local elites in the administration. Perhaps in the upstream regions of Egyptian Nubia, the local elites maintained a higher degree of autonomy, similar to the local rulers inside the Egyptian dominions in the Near East during the same phases (Morkot 2013: 914–19, 944–5). This factor may have had crucial consequences when Egyptian control over Nubia ended at the end of the second millennium BC.

In the last phase of the New Kingdom, relations between Egypt and African groups settled west of the Nile valley became increasingly important. Perhaps as a consequence of environmental changes taking place at the end of the second millennium BC, several groups living in the Western Desert started moving east in an attempt to enter the Nile valley (Morkot 2016a; 2016b: 258–60). Upon entering Egypt through the delta, they allied with other groups ravaging the Mediterranean coasts, the so-called Sea Peoples, who contributed to the crisis at the end of the Bronze Age and to the fall of important states such as the Hittite empire. Although some major attempts at mass migration may have been repeatedly repelled by the Egyptian rulers, Libyans were still able to enter the valley by infiltrating small groups and thanks to the Egyptian policy of using prisoners as labourers, and in this way they were incorporated into the Egyptian society. In particular, some of these Libyans became successful members of the army and, generation after generation, their families climbed the social ladder and entered the elite until eventually they ascended to the throne in the Third Intermediate Period (see also Section 3.2). Consequently, the relations with the Western Desert at the very end of the second millennium BC become as important as they were in the formative phases of the Egyptian civilization. Noteworthy also are the similar dynamics that may have taken place to the south of Egypt, in the Middle Nile valley, as suggested by the recently discovered fortress of Gala Abu Ahmed, in the Wadi Howar, whose establishment may date to the final phases of the Egyptian control of Nubia and which may have been intended to control a traditional route from the Western Desert into Upper Nubia (Jesse 2013) (Figure 14).

## 2.4 A Southern Path to the Royalty

The fact that in the troubled phase after the end of the New Kingdom the rulers of Egypt had their ultimate origin in the African regions around Egypt was not limited to the Libyans. A dynasty that emerged in the Middle Nile valley, which took control of Egypt after the Libyan dynasties, had Nubian lineage. Indeed, although recognizing the primacy of the Egyptian ruler, Nubian elites may have maintained their control over large tracts of the Middle Nile valley in the New Kingdom. With the end of Egyptian hegemony at the end of the second millennium BC, these areas (re-)gained full autonomy and transformed into independent polities (Morkot 2013: 950–1). The Nubian dynasty that ruled in Egypt may have emerged precisely in one of these polities.

The proposed interpretative model seems to fit with what we know from the archaeological evidence for the early first millennium BC. This includes two elite cemeteries, perhaps to be ascribed to the local aristocratic families controlling a couple of these independent polities in the Napata region at El-Kurru (Kendall 1999: 5–6) and Hillat el-Arab (Vincentelli 2006), and perhaps the names of some figures, who were most likely local rulers, that are known from monuments in Jebel Barkal and Kawa (Morkot 2000: 146–50). It is likely that since the very beginning these polities maintained links with Egypt and played a key

**Figure 14** The late New Kingdom and Napatan fortress of Gala Abu Ahmed in the Wadi Howar (Arachne-Eingabe © German Archaeological Institute and University of Cologne).

role in the management of the relations between Egypt and the southern regions (Morkot 2016b: 262–9). Despite the scarcity of textual sources, this role is shown by the gold objects found in the tombs at El-Kurru. These finds suggest that the people buried there maintained relations with some of the gold-bearing regions of Nubia, perhaps those between the Fourth and the Fifth Cataracts (Török 2009: 292). This hypothesis is supported by the evidence of gold extraction from the site of Hosh el-Guruf (Emberling & Williams 2010: 38). Other commodities from the cemetery of El-Kurru, such as obsidian, point to contacts with regions further south, Ethiopia and Eritrea being an obvious possibility (Török 2009: 312). While ivory may have been a crucial commodity in these exchanges (Morkot 2016: 266), the archaeological evidence is still scarce on this issue (Morkot 2000: 155), perhaps also because of its perishability. The occurrence of imported materials from the Near East at both Hillat el-Arab (Vincentelli 2006: 183–4) and El-Kurru (Heidorn 1994: 127–31) supports the hypothesis that the Upper Nubian elites were involved in a broad network of contacts. This role in the long-distance trade network may also have been a crucial factor in consolidating the political and economic influence of the Nubian elites.

Particularly important within these Nubian elites was the aristocratic family buried at El-Kurru, that, after unifying the Middle Nile regions under its control, also extended its influence to Egypt. Some of its members were the Twenty-Fifth Dynasty of Egypt in the list produced by Manetho, which is called 'Ethiopian'. This dynasty ruled in Egypt for about a century from ca. 750 BC until it was defeated by the Assyrians (Morkot 2000: 273–80). Noteworthy in this specific phase is the adoption of several traits of Egyptian origin by the Nubian elite, a process whose roots may lie in the earlier times when the Egyptian New Kingdom held control over Nubia. These traits were now an important factor of legitimation for the rule of the Twenty-Fifth Dynasty kings over Egypt (Section 3.3).

The involvement of the Upper Nubian elites in a broad network of contacts and exchanges also continued after the conquest of Egypt. Despite the fact that in the textual sources the military aspects of the relations between the Nile valley under the Nubian rule and the Assyrians were emphasized, it is highly likely that economic exchanges that were profitable for both sides were also taking place. An external source on the trade of commodities from Nubia to the Near East in this phase is represented by some Assyrian texts mentioning the 'horses of Kush', which is not surprising when we recall the penchant the Nubian aristocracy had for horses. This emerges from both the well-known passage of the victory stele of Pye, the Nubian ruler who conquered Egypt, where his disappointment upon finding starving horses in the stables of his enemy Nimlot is clear attestation, and from the discovery of tombs of horses in the cemetery at El-Kurru, where Pye, his predecessors and immediate successors were buried (Morkot 2000: 161–2).

The management of the flow of the African raw materials to Egypt, and to the Mediterranean and the Near East was of clear importance to the Nubian state as is confirmed by the Treasury, a monumental structure brought to light in Sanam, one of its main administrative centres, not far from the Jebel Barkal and Napata (Vincentelli 2011). This large and regular structure consisted of a central elongated courtyard delimited on three sides by modular squared rooms, which were probably storerooms, and possibly also had an upper floor (Figure 15). Recent investigations demonstrated that this was not only part of a larger area with administrative and storage facilities, but also yielded materials, including calcite vessels, faience objects and pottery imported from Egypt and the Near East. Alongside these finds were locally made gold and silver objects, raw materials, such as gold, ivory and ebony, all of which were possibly stored there ready to be exported to Egypt. Direct control over this structure by the state administration is demonstrated by the monumentality and regular plan of the building, and by the discovery of several sealings bearing the names of Twenty-Fifth Dynasty rulers and their immediate Napatan successors (Vincentelli 2006–7). The occurrence of objects of probable Nubian origin arriving from the Nile valley in pre-Aksumite

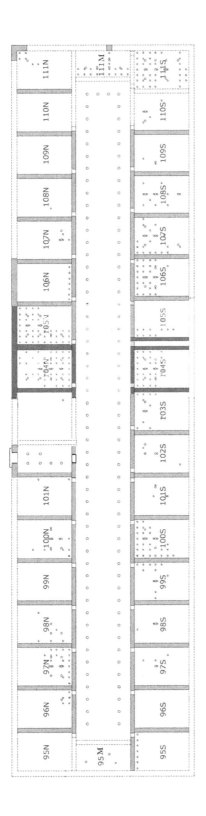

**Figure 15** Map of the Twenty-Fifth Dynasty and early Napatan Treasury in Sanam (© Sudanese–Italian Joint Expedition in the Napatan Region).

RESTORED MUD BRICK WALLS

MUD BRICK WALLS (RUINS, REMAINS)

contexts on the northern Ethio-Eritrean highlands, suggests that the exchange networks involving Napatan Nubia also extended to those regions, where many commodities were available (Manzo 1998: 39). It is nevertheless highly likely that in this phase the main route to the Near East and the Mediterranean that the raw materials from the Ethiopian-Eritrean highlands (ivory, most likely some ebony and aromatic resins) took was the trade network centred on South Arabia (Morkot 2016b: 264). This is suggested by the close cultural relations linking the African and Arabian regions of the southern Red Sea in the first half of the first millennium BC.

Therefore, all of this data highlights that the relations between Egypt and upstream regions continued after the end of the Twenty-Fifth Dynasty's control over Egypt, as the availability of African raw materials maintained its crucial status in both Egypt and in the Near East. Noteworthy are the similarities in this phase to the political and economic situation of north-eastern Africa in the first half of the second millennium BC. During that time, Egypt had to deal with another powerful state controlling the Middle Nile region and exercising a strong influence over the exchanges with the southern regions. This is suggested by the aforementioned finds of possible Nubian origin from northern Ethiopia and Eritrea, as well as the re-use of the Gala Abu Ahmed fortress in Napatan times, which may represent a node in the network of tracks crossing the Wadi Howar region, a natural route to the Ennedi and the Darfur (Jesse 2013). Therefore, it is perhaps not by a chance that, like in the first half of the second millennium BC, we also have evidence in this phase for Egyptian activities in the Red Sea. The resumption of activities in the Red Sea mainly emerges from the textual evidence of the Egyptian Twenty-Sixth Dynasty. This was perhaps conducted with the use of new types of ships and foreign sailors, and with the attempt to connect the Red Sea with the easternmost branch of the Nile delta by a channel at the time of Nekau II, in order to make possible a direct navigation between the river (and thus the Mediterranean) and the Red Sea (Lloyd 1977). Following the possible tensions in the earlier reign of Nekau II, a large military expedition was conducted by Psamtek II against Nubia at the very beginning of the sixth century BC. This expedition may ultimately have been an attempt at gaining command over the Middle Nile networks (Török 2009: 361–2). Regardless of their aims, these Egyptian efforts both on the Red Sea and in the Nile valley were seemingly unsuccessful. Similar attempts may have also characterized the Achaemenid policy towards the African neighbours of Egypt. This is perhaps the reasoning behind the plans for the invasion of the Middle Nile regions reported by Herodotus (Török 2009: 364), and the completion of the canal between the Nile and the Red Sea to reach Persia and perhaps also the regions of the southern Red Sea (Klotz 2015). Be that as it may, these efforts were once again unsuccessful and the control of the Middle Nile and the flow of commodities crossing it firmly remained in the hands of the Nubians. The Nubians also provided ivory and ebony to the Achaemenid rulers, as well as also troops for their attempted invasion of Greece. Artefacts from the Napatan elite tombs at Meroe and some textual sources suggest that diplomatic relations were established between the Nubian and Persian rulers (Morkot 1991: 331–2). Indeed, it is highly probable that in this phase the exchange of African commodities continued to be closely intertwined with diplomacy (see Section 3.1).

## 2.5 From Peripheries to Centres

The fact that elaborate tombs containing prized objects to be ascribed to individuals related to the royal court are found not only in the Napata-Jebel Barkal area, where the Napatan royal cemetery was located, but also at Meroe, is not surprising. Meroe had certainly been an important administrative centre of the Nubian kingdom since the Twenty-Fifth Dynasty and this continued later into the Napatan period (Török 1997: 128–30). It was suggested that the importance of Meroe may have been somehow favoured by the aforementioned expedition conducted by Psamtek II against Nubia. This expedition may have proven that the Napata region was too exposed to potential threats arriving from the north. Nevertheless, in the third century BC, the shift of the political centre of gravity of the Nubian state to its southernmost administrative node marked by the establishment of the royal cemetery at Begrawiya, not far from Meroe, remains largely unexplained. It should be remarked that this shift was also associated with the flourishing of the Butana, the region around Meroe, where several settlements were established. Furthermore, the shift was associated with the introduction of deities that were most likely rooted in the Butana area into the Meroitic pantheon and with the use of the Meroitic language and script in official written documents, which largely replaced the Egyptian language and hieroglyphics that up until this time had been used for all inscriptions (Török 1997: 62, 436–7, 500–5). All of these elements suggest an increased importance and central role of the southern part of the Nubian state during this period, which is labelled as the Meroitic phase.

It should also be stressed that in the Meroitic phase both textual and archaeological data indicate that relations with Egypt held continued importance. This was not only the case with the cultural links, which continued with reference to the earlier Egyptian traditions, but also to the Ptolemaic innovations (Section 3.3). It is also certain that the political and economic connections between Egypt and the Middle Nile regions were very close. Indeed, the 'geographic' texts of Hellenistic and Roman times extensively describe the regions of north-eastern Africa paying close attention to their mineral, animal and vegetal resources, and this clearly shows how and why these were considered important in the Mediterranean perspective (Török 1997: 71–3). Indeed, the imports from the Mediterranean discovered in contexts related to the Meroitic court (Török 1989) and the concentrations of African raw materials, such as the ivory tusks and ebony rods, from the palace of Queen Amanishakheto found at Wad ben Naga (Vercoutter 1962: 280–1) (Figure 16) suggest that, like in the previous phases, these economic exchanges continued to be crucial for the Nubian state. They were most likely important for their economic value, and because the imported materials were also used in the internal redistributive network to maintain the ties between the court and the local elites, and between the centre and peripheries (Edwards 1996: 46–7). In this perspective it should be noted that the Meroitic state may have been a 'Sudanic state' – a type of state that is also well known from later examples

**Figure 16** Ivory and ebony rods in a storeroom of the palace of the first century AD Meroitic queen Amanishakheto at Wad Ben Naga (© Section Française de la Direction des Antiquités du Soudan).

in the Shaelian belt – whose prosperity was mainly based on the control of long-distance trade and thus on the ability of the rulers to obtain raw materials through exchanges and raids into their peripheries, and to manage trade (Edwards 1996: 20–2). The Meroitic state, which was rooted in the Nile valley, had also extended its influence to inland areas, as it included pastoral mobile groups. Therefore, this state was in control of the natural resources available at its fringes, which were highly sought-after in the Mediterranean.

It should be stressed that in this specific phase the list of African commodities that were highly desired in Egypt and the Mediterranean was enlarged to also include live elephants. Indeed, this was the consequence of the Indian expedition conducted by Alexander the Great that led to the military use of elephants to be extended to the Mediterranean. They then became essential components of Hellenistic armies, as well as symbols of royalty as a consequence of Alexander's symbolic status across the whole ancient world (Scullard 1974: 64–76). In particular, the Ptolemies ruling over Egypt after the untimely death of Alexander were eager to acquire African elephants for their army because they were cut off from direct access to Indian elephants by the hostility of their one-time allies, the Seleucids. Initially, this may have led to attempts at getting elephants via the Nile valley, but nevertheless this solution was very soon abandoned, perhaps also because of the hostility of the Meroitic rulers, who directly controlled the Middle Nile regions. This situation may have stimulated the organization of state-run expeditions along the Red Sea with direct access to regions where elephants could be obtained. For this reason several outposts and harbours were established at that time along the African coast of the Red Sea (Casson 1993). The use of the Red Sea also continued in later Ptolemaic times, when the interest in getting African elephants to be trained as war-machines declined after they were demonstrated to be quite ineffective in the battle of Raphia between Ptolemy IV and Antiochus III (Scullard 1974: 139–45).

Also noteworthy in this phase is the combined use of the Red Sea and the Nile valley routes to get African commodities. It is perhaps not by chance that after the Roman conquest of Egypt, the imperial policy towards the Middle Nile valley was also closely linked to the one established for the Red Sea. The war between the Romans and Meroites at the time of Augustus was caused by the attempt to impose Roman influence on Lower Nubia and perhaps also more southern regions, yet it broke up while most of the Roman troops controlling Egypt were taking part in a military expedition to Arabia Felix, a region in Southern Arabia famous for its incense, and commanding the southern entrance of the Red Sea from the east (Török 2009: 427–42). The Meroitic presence on the southern border of Egypt may also have been regarded by the Romans as particularly dangerous, especially when considering the recurring riots taking place in Upper Egypt in this phase. After an in-depth Roman military expedition into Meroitic territory, the war was ended by a peace agreement, which recognized Meroitic independence and sanctioned the division of Lower Nubia into two areas of influence.

The increasing activities in the southern Red Sea certainly led to more direct relations between the groups inhabiting those regions and Egypt from the third century BC onwards. This was likely the case with the groups inhabiting the African coast and the inland regions, as some of the textual sources suggest (Burstein 1989). Despite being an admittedly limited archaeological dataset, due to the few archaeological explorations conducted mainly in the coastal area of Sudan and Eritrea, the material culture evidence also supports the case for contact between Egypt and those regions. This is suggested by some glass beads from Ptolemaic-early Roman Egypt found in tombs in the inland region of Aksum (Figure 17). Indeed, a consequence of the trade activities in the southern Red Sea was certainly an increasing involvement in the exchanges of African commodities by the polities located in those areas, like the one emerging in the Aksum region, on the Ethiopia highland, at the end of the first millennium BC (Manzo 2005: 54–5). In terms of the changing relations between Egypt and

**Figure 17** Mosaic glass beads imported from Ptolemaic or Early Roman Egypt from an elite tomb at Ona Enda Aboi Zewge, near Aksum (© 'L'Orientale', ISMEO and Boston University Joint Expedition at Aksum).

Africa during the Hellenistic phase, the aforementioned shift of the Nubian state's centre of gravity to the south may well be explained by the need to exercise more direct and efficient control over the regions on its southern fringes, where new polities were forming and many highly desired commodities were available. Indeed, this shift may have been an attempt to avoid the marginalization of the Nile valley route in favour of the increasingly exploited Red Sea trade route.

## 2.6 Egypt and Africa in Broader Horizons

After the Roman conquest of Egypt, and the discovery of the seasonal monsoon winds by Graeco-Egyptian sailors, the Red Sea started to become part of a longer and more articulate route leading to the Gulf and India, which was described in full in the mid-first century AD in *Periplus of the Erythrean Sea*, a commercial handbook for tradesman (Casson 1989). In the meantime, the Red Sea always was an alternative, and complementary, route to the southern regions instead of the more traditional route via the Nile valley. The trade route to India enhanced the central importance of the Eritrean coast and its hinterland not only as suppliers of some of the commodities traditionally exported to Egypt and the rest of the Mediterranean, such as ivory, ebony and aromatic resins, but also as a node in a network through which spices produced in the Indian peninsula and silk from the Far East were obtained. In this general context, the ports on the Egyptian Red Sea coast also became crucial to the movement of these goods, as they represented the western terminal of the network.

Returning to north-eastern Africa, it should be stressed that in the first centuries AD, there were two southern counterparts to Roman Egypt: the Nubian state centred on Meroe in the Middle Nile and the Aksumite State on the southern Red Sea, centred on Aksum in the Ethio-Eritrean highlands. This kingdom very likely emerged in the last centuries of the first millennium BC, yet in the mid-first century AD *Periplus of the Erythrean Sea* tells us that the kingdom had extended its influence to the Eritrean coast, where the important port of Adulis was located (Casson 1989: 52, § 4–6). The Aksumite kingdom may have reached a peak of its power between the late third and the fourth century AD. In that phase, in the mid-fourth century AD, Christianity was also adopted as the state religion by king Ezana (Phillipson 2012: 74–8). Although the archaeological evidence suggests that the Aksumite kingdom was part of a broad network also reaching the Near East and the western provinces of the Roman empire (Manzo 2005), most of these relations were taking place via Roman Egypt, as also attested by the long-lasting close doctrinal and hierarchical ties between the Aksumite Christianism and the patriarchate of Alexandria (Phillipson 2012: 94–5). As the adoption of Christianity shows, traits of Mediterranean culture were widely adopted in those phases in the Ethio-Eritrean highlands, as did the use of Greek in official royal inscriptions and in the legends of the coins that had occurred sometime before the adoption of Christianity (Manzo 1998: 40–1, 47).

The role of the Aksumite kingdom as supplier of African commodities to the Roman Mediterranean largely overlapped with that traditionally played by the Napatan-Meroitic kingdom. The connection between the exchange network centred on Meroe converging on the Nile and the other focussed on the Red Sea and centred on Aksum was also very evident in ancient times, as it emerged in earlier sections. Considering this connection and the similarities between the commodities traded along the two routes, there was potential for competition between Aksum and Meroe, the two powers controlling their southern terminals. Nevertheless, at this current stage of our knowledge we do not have any clear evidence of any direct competition between the two in the archaeological and textual record. The fourth century Aksumite military intervention in the Middle Nile valley, which certainly touched Meroe, may have been more related to the Aksumite attempts at preventing the Noba groups that entered the Meroitic territories from compromising security on the western Aksumite border than to the will of subduing the Nubian kingdom (Hatke 2013: 57–80, but see contra Török 1997: 483–4). From this perspective, it should be stressed that the emergence and ascent of Aksumite power between the very end of the first millennium BC and the beginning of the first millennium AD did not prevent the Meroitic kingdom from experiencing a very prosperous phase, which is evident in its impressive architectural and artistic achievements in the first century AD (Török 1997: 461–4). Moreover, in the mid-third century, the Meroitic kingdom was able to take control over the northern part of Lower Nubia following the withdrawal of the Roman frontier to the Syene/Aswan area (Török 1997: 475). Yet, imports from the Mediterranean continued to find their way via Egypt into Middle Nile contexts and this suggests that Aksumite activity did not have an impact on the involvement of the Meroites in long-distance exchanges, which may have been crucial for the economic prosperity and political stability of their state (Section 2.5).

It was only in the late third and fourth century AD that the first evidence of a crisis in the Meroitic kingdom can be found. This crisis may be related on one hand to the political instability affecting Meroe's main political and economic partner (i.e. the Roman empire) in those phases. On the other hand, the period was marked by increasing raids by the peoples of the inland regions east and west of the Nile valley who not only threatened the caravan routes crossing the deserts, but also the administrative and urban centres in the Nile valley, in Egypt and possibly even in the Meroitic kingdom (Török 1997: 476–83). In particular, continuing over a long period of time, the threats to the caravan routes may have compromised both the economy of the Meroitic state, and also its internal cohesion. Therefore, the Aksumite military campaigns in the first half of the fourth century AD in the Middle Nile valley and in the Eastern Desert aimed at protecting the north-western fringes of the Aksumite sphere of influence threatened by the groups coming from the deserts. The campaigns may also have been aimed at keeping some of the land routes linking Aksum to Egypt via the Eastern Desert safe (Hatke 2013: 59–61). However, the core areas of the Aksumite kingdom may have been protected from the raids by peoples from the deserts thanks to their location in remote regions of the Ethio-Eritrean highlands.

Aksum largely occupied the economic and political vacuum left by the crisis of the Meroitic kingdom, which was to the detriment of the international importance of the Middle Nile regions. The scarcity of imports from the Mediterranean and Egypt in Upper Nubia and in the region of Meroe after the fourth century AD suggests that these areas were largely isolated from trade with Egypt. The only notable exception is represented by Lower Nubia, where a new kingdom called Noubadia arose. From a certain point onwards this new kingdom became a federate of the Roman Empire, an ally supporting the defence of the southern frontier of Egypt (Török 1997: 485). It was precisely this newly established polity that represented the gateway to Africa in Late Antique Egypt, as it established intense relations with the Roman empire (Török 2009: 530, 539–40). Perhaps at that time Noubadia was acting as an exclusive middleman in regional exchanges. This is suggested by the large number of Roman imports in the cemeteries of the Noubadian elite at Qustul and Ballana. It is noteworthy that Noubadian trade may have been oriented not only towards the regions upstream of Lower Nubia, but also towards the regions lying to the south-west of Lower Nubia, that could be reached by the caravan trade across the Western Desert. This trade was now possible through the increasing use of the camel as a beast of burden, an animal that was much more physiologically suitable for the terrain and conditions of the Western Desert than the donkey. Although its earliest evidence on the southern fringes of Egypt date to the early first millennium BC, camel was very slowly and gradually adopted in north-eastern Africa, and came to be more widely used only during the Hellenistic and Roman periods (Rowley-Conwy 1988).

The regions south of Lower Nubia only gradually re-entered the networks involving Egypt and the Mediterranean. In cultural and ideological terms the resumption of relations with Egypt and the Mediterranean by the regions of the

Middle Nile is also shown by the adoption of Christianity in the sixth century AD, a process which was connected to the establishment of close political and diplomatic relations with the Roman Empire (Welsby 2002: 31–4). Further evidence is seen in the Nubian troops who formed part of the Roman imperial contribution to the South Arabian expedition undertaken by the Aksumite king Kaleb in the first half of the sixth century AD (Welsby 2002: 19). Therefore, this phase bears similarities to the earlier periods, when both the states of the Middle Nile valley and the ones of the Ethio-Eritrean highlands functioned as the partners of Egypt (and indirectly of the Mediterranean) in the trade networks. The aforementioned Aksumite military expedition to South Arabia once again shows the close links between the interactions taking place along the Nile valley and the ones on the Red Sea, which at that time was the westernmost branch of the broader network of the Indian Ocean. Indeed, although officially undertaken to protect the Christian communities in South Arabia against the persecution by the Himyaritic kings who had embraced Judaism, the campaign led by Kaleb was probably promoted to avoid the Sassanid expansion into the southern Red Sea (Phillipson 2012: 203–6). This objective was only provisionally achieved, as the Sassanids were later on able to occupy not only South Arabia but also Egypt itself in 619 AD (Welsby 2002: 68).

In a mere few years, the Arab expansion radically changed the whole international situation and the networks linking Egypt and its African neighbours. A new universal religion, Islam, and a shared language, Arabic, were progressively expanding in Egypt and within its neighbours. The only notable exception was the Aksumite kingdom and its successor, which remained Christian. These circumstances certainly favoured interactions, as did the wide adoption of the camel as a means of transport and travel, which intensified the relations with the inland desert regions as well as the regions far beyond the inhospitable desert lands, to a degree that had perhaps not been achieved since the first half of the Holocene, before the start of the aridification process mentioned earlier (Section 1.2). But the control over all the network was once again in the hands of who was controlling its northern terminal, Egypt, to the detriment of the regions south of it.

## 3 Africans in Egypt, Egyptians in Africa

### 3.1 Modes of Interaction: Migrations, Conquests, Trade and Diplomacy

In several periods of the long history of relations between Egypt and its African neighbours we have traces of the presence of individuals or groups of people from other African regions in Egypt. Moreover, some centres and regions can be regarded as true interfaces between Egypt and Africa, not only because they were intensively exposed to such kinds of dynamics as a result of their geographic position, but also because they most likely had a mixed population. This was the case, for example, with the Dakhla oasis in the Western Desert, and of the region of the First Cataract. In late Old Kingdom times, Dakhla was part of the Egyptian state, with an administrative centre, production areas and a cemetery featuring some large mastabas of the local governors (Kaper & Willems 2002). However, the Egyptians were not the only inhabitants of the area as local people were also present, as the archaeological remains suggest (Hope 2002: 50–1). Moreover, considering the fact that the Dakhla oasis may have constituted a true hub in that period, a place traversed by routes crossing the Western Desert (Section 2.2), Egyptians, the local people and also groups and individuals from remote regions of the desert and different sectors of the Nile valley may have passed through the area. In the case of Elephantine and its surroundings, which traditionally represent the southern limit of Egypt, this area was most likely inhabited both by Egyptians and Nubians since the earliest phases of occupation. That these two groups were living together is suggested on the basis of the archaeological evidence (Gatto 2009: 128, 132). Nubian ceramic materials have constantly been found in the excavated settlement of Elephantine, although they do not outnumber the Egyptian objects, which form the majority of the materials (Raue 2019) (Figure 18). Further cases of settlements and regions where Nubians were a permanent element of the local population since very ancient periods may have occurred in Upper Egypt (Ejsmond 2019: 35–6).

These cases refer to prolonged and constant contact in frontier areas, porous areas of interaction where different group identities traditionally meet and cultural processes of integration and entanglement were naturally taking place (Török 2009: 7–8). However, there is also evidence of attempts by numerous groups of people to migrate to the Egyptian Nile valley. In this case, the evidence is often represented by texts, which obviously express the attitude of the Egyptian state towards these people. The more evident and perhaps most famous case is the repeated attempts by apparently large groups from the Western Desert to enter the Egyptian Nile valley at the end of the New Kingdom (Section 2.3). This dynamic may have its origins in the environmental changes that pushed the groups inhabiting the Western Desert to move towards the Nile, as had happened in earlier periods of history, such as in the first half of the Holocene, when possible movements towards the valley can be reconstructed through archaeological evidence (Section 2.1). After the formation of the Egyptian state, the usual reaction to such migrations was military in nature, which is what clearly emerges from the textual sources. The texts show the typical effects of an ideological polarization between Egypt and the Desert with its inhabitants. Furthermore, this polarization equates the opposition between

**Figure 18** A Nubian cooking vessel from an assemblage dating to 2450–2150
BC at Elephantine (courtesy Dietrich Raue).

Egypt and the Desert to the contrast between Order, as embodied by the ruler,
and Chaos, embodied by otherness of the foreigners. Archaeology confirms that
in the Nineteenth Dynasty a defence and monitoring system was put in place in
the area to the west of the Delta (Snape 2013: 441–2), to deter the potentially
massive attempts at entering the valley that were taking place (Morkot 2016a:
31–2). Such moves may have taken place not only in Egypt but also in regions
under the Egyptian control further to the south. The fortress of Gala Abu Ahmed
in the Wadi Howar in the Nubian Western Desert, the establishment of which
dates to the end of the New Kingdom, may be an example of similar concerns
resulting in the construction of defensive infrastructures (Section 2.3). It
remains possible that while the main migratory waves may have been repelled,
movements of smaller groups may have passed through unnoticed or were
tolerated. A similar situation of migrations into territories under Egyptian
control, but this time taking the form of movements of smaller groups, is also
recorded in the Semna Despatches, dating to the reign of Amenemhat III, at the
end of the Twelfth Dynasty. These despatches were sent by the commanders of
the fortress of Semna, at the southern end of the Second Cataract, which at that
time marked the Egyptian Nubian frontier. The commanders sent them to the
central state administration, to report on the situation at the border, during
a period characterized by both antagonism and also intense trade with Upper
Nubia (Section 2.2). Of course, being archival documents and not texts directly

related to the royal monuments, the ideological conditioning is less evident in these texts. A despatch records an approach on the Egyptian frontier by a group of Medjaw, most likely arriving from the Eastern Desert. They were apparently pushed to do so by a famine affecting inland regions. The famine itself came in the wake of general environmental changes that led to more arid conditions in the Nubian-Sudanese regions away from the Nile valley (Section 1.2). In the first half of the second millennium BC, the appearance of new unprecedented cultural traits in the archaeological record of the Nile valley, both in Egypt, Lower Nubia and more southern regions, which do not have a local origin, like the Pan-Grave culture, may be related to such kinds of dynamics (de Souza 2018: 148–9). In all these cases both the archaeological and textual sources show that new components were appearing in the Egyptian Nile valley: this demonstrates that, despite textual sources that often pretend the migratory movements to the Egyptian Nile valley had failed, these attempts were in fact frequently successful. They very often resulted in cultural entanglement and hybridization (see Section 3.3).

Moreover, it should be stressed that if the Egyptian state was generally trying to control the attempts at entering the areas under its administration, sometimes it may have on the contrary favoured such dynamics. This is the case with groups of people who were appreciated for their skills, such as the soldiers mentioned in the Egyptian textual sources from the late Old Kingdom onwards. According to his 'biographic' inscription, Weni led the army in a successful Palestinian campaign under the reign of Pepy I, and this army included troops from several regions of Nubia and the Western Desert (Section 2.2). However, it is not known how these recruits entered the Egyptian army, whether they arrived by themselves in Egypt of their own free will or whether they were conscripted after following Egyptian exped-itions on their way back, as was the case of the recruits from the land of Yam, who were escorting Harkhuf during his return from his third journey (see Section 2.2). This specific kind of interaction is also repeatedly recorded in later phases: in the First Intermediate Period several inscriptions of Nubian soldiers, were found in the region of Gebelein (see Section 3.2) (Figure 19), while in the Eleventh Dynasty we know that Nubians were recruited in Lower Nubia, as stated in the inscriptions of the Nubian soldier Tjehemau, who may have been recruited during a visit by King Mentuhotep II to the region (Darnell 2003: 33, 35). Within the framework of the previously described actions to prevent mass invasions from the Western Desert at the end of the second millennium BC, the Egyptian state may have decided pragmatically to allow some groups to settle in the valley in exchange for their service in the army (Morkot 2016a: 31–32).

**Figure 19** First Intermediate Period funerary stelae of Nubian soldiers from Gebelein (from *Kush*. 9, courtesy National Corporation for Antiquities and Museums).

Occasionally, there may have been circumstances that resulted in Africans being present in Egypt that were caused by military expeditions. We can assume that these may have been raids rather than expeditions aimed at settling permanently in the Egyptian Nile valley, such as the one described in the Second Intermediate Period inscription by Sebeknakht at El Kab (Section 2.3,

Figure 13), or the raids conducted by both the Nubians and the Blemmyes who were mainly ravaging Upper Egypt in Late Antique times (Section 2.6). Although, of course, such dynamics are mainly described in the textual sources, some specific artefacts may have connections to these military expeditions: this is the case with a calcite vessel bearing the name of Sebeknakht, a governor of Hierakonpolis. This vessel was found at Kerma, which is probably the capital city of the kingdom of Kush, and may have been looted during a Kushite raid in the Second Intermediate Period (Anderson & Welsby 2004: 101; Davies 2003: 53, note 3). Furthermore, the Middle Kingdom Egyptian statues, made to be consecrated in tombs and temples of Middle and Upper Egypt and found in Second Intermediate Period monuments at Kerma, may have found their way to the capital of Kush in similar circumstances (Valbelle 2004; 2011: 13). Similarly, some objects that were probably looted from churches found in the Noubadian royal tombs at Ballana in Lower Nubia may result from the afore-mentioned raids of the Egyptian Nile valley that were taking place in the fourth and fifth century AD (Török 1988: 138–43). In the cases of the raids conducted by the Blemmyans and Noubadae in Late Antique times, the goal was certainly to simply get hold of booty and to loot. Indeed, raiding may be regarded as a very important economic and social activity for those peoples. In the case of the Second Intermediate Period Kushite raids, a more complex political and military goal can be glimpsed, as at that time Kush was an important ally of the Hyksos rulers in the fight against the Thebans for the control of Egypt (Section 2.3). Perhaps a more complex political and military goal can be glimpsed also for the Meroitic raids in the last decades of the first century BC, following the establishment of the border between the Meroitic kingdom and the Roman empire after the Roman conquest of Egypt (Section 2.5). Indeed, we cannot exclude that in this case the Meroitic rulers were somehow hoping to gain an advantage from the riots taking place in Upper Egypt and in the Roman-controlled northern part of Lower Nubia, with the possible aim of changing the political and administrative setting of that region (Török 2009: 441). Also noteworthy is the archaeological trace of this specific circumstance in the form of the famous bronze head of Augustus found ritually buried under the threshold of a temple at Meroe, which may have been looted on the occasion of those military clashes (Török 1989–1990: 181–2) (Figure 20).

Similarly, some Egyptian military expeditions conducted into the neighbour-ing African regions may merely have been simple raids, as was suggested in the case of the expedition of the Fourth Dynasty king Snefru recorded in the Palermo Stone and dating circa 2600 BC. This expedition was conducted to the southern regions, possibly to Upper Nubia if the large number of seized livestock, making Lower Nubia and the desert regions less likely, is trustworthy

(Jiménez-Serrano 2006). Although other Egyptian military expeditions probably did not aim at establishing long-lasting control over specific regions, they certainly had political and military aims other than solely to loot: this may have been the case for the expedition conducted by Psamtek II at the beginning of the sixth century BC, which perhaps took place as part of the efforts to weaken the Napatan state in the Middle Nile valley and to establish more direct links with the areas where the sources of commodities were located (Section 2.4). If the traditional hypothesis can be accepted that it was on that very occasion that the monuments of the Twenty-Fifth Dynasty Nubian rulers and their immediate Napatan successors were systematically and almost ritually damaged in the temples of Dukki Gel, near Kerma, and Jebel Barkal (Bonnet & Valbelle 2003: 770–1), then this may well confirm the hypothesis that the expedition had a specific political goal (Figure 21). It is interesting that on that occasion foreigners were also members of the Egyptian expeditionary corps, as shown by the graffiti left by Greek-Carian soldiers on the legs of the colossal statues of

**Figure 20** Bronze head of Roman emperor Augustus found at Meroe (© The Trustees of the British Museum).

Rameses II carved on the façade of the Abu Simbel temple (Eide et al. 1994: 286–90). These graffiti were left during a phase in which the involvement of Phoenicians and Greek sailors in Egyptian activities conducted on the Red Sea was highly likely (Section 2.4). Therefore, these expeditions not only led to the presence of Egyptians in other African regions, but also of individuals and groups who come via Egypt from even more distant areas.

In several other cases military expeditions certainly resulted in the long-term occupation of specific regions, in the settlement of administrators, the military and sometimes priests and labour groups. The most evident case related to the presence of large numbers of Egyptians in the neighbouring African regions is represented by the establishment of administrative centres, outposts or

0                                  100cm

**Figure 21** Cachette of damaged statues of the Twenty-Fifth Dynasty rulers and their Napatan successors in the temple of Dukki Gel, near Kerma (© Mission Suisse-Franco-Soudanaise de Kerma/Doukki Gel).

fortresses in the areas that came to enter the sphere of Egyptian political influence. In Nubia this took place from the Old Kingdom onwards and became more intense in the Middle and New Kingdom (Sections 2.2, 2.3) leading to the establishment of communities of Egyptian officials and soldiers. Similar processes may also have taken place in the oases. These Egyptian communities stayed for long periods of time, or even permanently in foreign regions. This is particularly evident in Lower Nubia in the late Middle Kingdom and in both Lower and Upper Nubia in the New Kingdom (Smith 2003: 74–96), but also at Dakhla in the late Old Kingdom (Kaper & Willems 2002). This led to the rise of expatriate communities. Indeed, the fact that expatriate communities were formed is shown by the occurrence of Egyptian cemeteries in these regions. It is certain that these expatriate communities were interacting with the local inhabitants in the regions where the Egyptian settlements were located (see Section 3.2). From this perspective, the establishment of Twenty-Fifth Dynasty political influence over Egypt in the mid-eighth century BC (Section 2.4), also had similar consequences, although in this case only small groups of Nubians or single persons were settling in Egypt and there is no evidence of the establishment of new centres. The settlement of Nubian dignitaries – often with a priestly rank – mainly in the Theban area of Egypt is a notable case, the more obvious example being the Nubian princess and 'God's Wife of Amun', Amenirdis (Morkot 2013: 956–7, 961–3).

A further way that small groups and single individuals may have entered and even settled in Egypt with the permission of the Egyptian state is through the diplomatic exchanges and other dynamics taking place between the Egyptian elite and the elites of its African neighbours. We are informed that at least by the reign of the Sixth Dynasty king Merenra meetings between the Egyptian and Nubian rulers were taking place in the First Cataract region (Török 2009: 60). The intensity of those relations is perhaps reflected in the adoption of loyalist names by some members of Nubian ruling families at the end of the Old Kingdom. Indeed, their names sometimes contained the name of an Egyptian ruler, such as in the case of the Nubian named Teti-ankh, as mentioned in the execration texts dating to that phase (Osing 1976: 142). The Thirteenth Dynasty papyrus Boulaq 18 describes the presence of a group of Medjaw in the Egyptian royal court, which has been interpreted as a diplomatic delegation, but may also refer to suppliers of commodities for a royal festival (Liszka & de Souza 2020: 240). Later on, the stele of Kamose informs us that diplomatic envoys were also moving from the Hyksos capital to Kush at the end of the Second Intermediate Period: one of these was captured by the Thebans on the 'route of the Oasis' (Section 2.3). In the New Kingdom, the representation of a Nubian princess on a chariot in the scene of the presentation of the Nubian tribute in the tomb of Huy, dating to the time of

Tutankhamon (Section 2.3, Figure 4), may even suggest that the Egyptian rulers may also have adopted with Nubia practices well known in the context of their interactions with the Near Eastern partners, like the diplomatic wedding (Morkot 2000: 85–7). Indeed, similar to their Near Eastern counterparts, African princesses may also have had to join the royal harem as a means of consolidating relations between the Egyptian ruler and the Nubian elites, although the relation between the two spheres may have been very unbalanced in that specific phase. With regard to the later phases one of the most obvious cases of diplomatic interaction and of the presence of ambassadors from Egypt (although possibly not Egyptians) in other African regions is the embassy sent by Cambyses to the Napatan king described by Herodotus. In the case of diplomatic exchanges at the time of the Twenty-Seventh Dynasty, their material trace may have survived in an elite tomb dating to the Napatan phase in the South cemetery at Meroe. This evidence consists of a *rython* vessel with an elaborate pedestal representing an Amazon upon which a scene representing a victory of the Persians over the Greeks is painted, which was possibly made in Ionia (i.e. in a culturally Greek area under the Persian political control) (Török 1989: 69). Indeed, this high-quality vessel may have been a diplomatic gift to the Napatan ruler from the Persian court. In one of the later royal Meroitic tombs, a high-quality silver vessel decorated with a scene perhaps representing Augustus as a just judge, which would fit well with the Roman imperial propaganda, may also have been a diplomatic gift (Török 1989–1990: 182–3), perhaps exchanged on the occasion of the diplomatic interactions following the cease of military conflict between Rome and Meroe during the time of Augustus (Section 2.5). It should be stressed that we also know from textual sources that on that occasion Meroitic ambassadors were moving through Egypt and presumably Alexandria to Samos, where they met Augustus. During later times, the southernmost Latin inscription from Musawwarat es-Sufra can be ascribed to a third century AD Roman ambassador to a Meroitic queen (Łajtar & van der Vliet 2006) (Figure 22), while epigraphic traces of the passage of the Meroitic envoys to Roman Egypt are known from the temple of Isis in Philae (Eide et al.1998: 1000–10, 1024–31). Indeed, at that time the temple of Isis in Philae held a crucial role in the diplomatic relations and in maintaining peace at the border between Roman Egypt and Meroitic kingdom (Török 2009: 467–9). Of course, in this case diplomacy was bound up with religion, as remained the case up until Late Antiquity. This is shown by the fact that the conversion of Nubia to Christianity took place within the framework of diplomatic missions sent to the regions south of Egypt by the imperial court in Constantinople in the sixth century AD. Furthermore, the Aksumite rulers own conversion to Christianity may have followed an intense period of economic and political interaction with the Roman empire (Section 2.6). Some objects from elite tombs in Lower Nubia, such as an

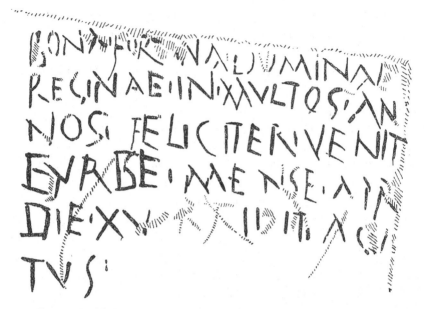

**Figure 22** Third century AD Latin inscription of a Roman envoy from Musawwarat es-Sufra (from *Kush* 12, courtesy National Corporation for Antiquities and Museums).

alabaster dish from the fifth century AD with a representation of two emperors, may have been produced in the workshops working for the imperial court at Constantinople (Deichmann 1966). If this is the case then it may represent material evidence of the diplomatic relations that led to the alliance between the empire and the Noubadae and ultimately to their own conversion to Christianity.

Similar to the well-known exchanges of commodities that took place in the framework of diplomatic relations in the late Bronze Age Near East (see Liverani 1990), diplomatic and political relations between Egypt and its African neighbours may have been related to exchanges of commodities and state-administered trade. Indeed, the repeated Egyptian expeditions aimed at acquiring commodities and raw materials were very often intertwined with diplomacy. In this case, of course, we are dealing with very brief visits to the involved region, which can be identified both on the basis of references in the Egyptian sources, such as in the case of the expeditions led by Harkhuf at the end of the Sixth Dynasty (Section 2.2), or in the case of the maritime expedition to the land of Punt during the reign of Hatshepsut (Section 2.3). Given the perishable nature of most of the exchanged commodities it is unsurprising that only very rarely did these expeditions leave material traces. The discovery at Kerma of a locally made stone stela bearing the inscription with the names of two Egyptian boat-captains dating to the end of the Old Kingdom may suggest that those two officials were leading a diplomatic-trade mission, perhaps similar to the ones described by Harkhuf and other officials of the Sixth Dynasty (Figure 23). Moreover, some royal and private Egyptian statues found at Kerma may have been donated to the local ruler or consecrated in local temples on the occasion of some of these missions (Valbelle 2011: 13).

As far as the close connection between trade and diplomacy goes, the expedition to the land of Punt of the time of Hatshepsut provides a case in point. The link between trade and diplomacy can be clearly seen in part of the reliefs representing the exchange of commodities between the leader of the Egyptian mission and the local ruler and his family (Espinel 2011: 350–3). These close ties between trade and diplomacy may have continued also in the first millennium BC, when the direct involvement of the royal courts of the polities south of Egypt in long-distance exchanges was pointed out (Section 2.4). After the Roman occupation of Egypt, the role of private entrepreneurs became crucial in long-distance trade on the Roman-Egyptian side (see e.g. Sidebotham 1986: 78–112). On the contrary, with regard to the African policies south of Egypt at that time, long-distance trade may have been largely managed by the elites or, to be more precise, by the rulers, as has been suggested on archaeological grounds in the case of the Meroitic state (Edwards 1996: 46–7), and as can also be suggested on the basis of both the archaeological and textual sources for the Aksumite kingdom (Manzo 2005).

Indeed, also on such occasions like military expeditions, the Egyptians may have been accompanied by foreigners. At Mersa/Wadi Gawasis, the harbour on the Egyptian Red Sea coast from where the maritime expeditions to the land of Punt were launched in Middle Kingdom times (Section 2.2), some Levantine and Minoan ceramics were discovered. It was therefore suggested that members of the Levantine communities living in Egypt were taking part in these enterprises (Bard & Fattovich 2018: 180–1). These expatriate communities were mainly located in the eastern Nile Delta, and the one settled at Avaris-Tell el-Daba is certainly the most widely known of these. Interestingly, the site at Mersa/Wadi Gawasis also provided evidence of the involvement of Nubians, perhaps from Nubian communities in Egypt, in the expeditions to Punt (Manzo 2010). Similar involvement of foreigners in the Egyptian maritime activities in the Red Sea is well known at the time of the Twenty-Sixth Dynasty (Section 2.4).

## 3.2 Stories of Success and Integration

All of the modes of interaction described led to the presence of Egyptians in neighbouring African regions as well as of African foreigners in Egypt.

**Figure 23** Local stela with a cursive hieroglyphic inscription mentioning two Egyptian boat-captains of the end of the Old Kingdom from Kerma (© Mission Suisse-Franco-Soudanaise de Kerma/Doukki Gel).

Despite the highly polarized perspective emerging from the texts, in which Egyptians and foreigners are regarded as two completely distinct and separate entities, daily interactions between the different groups resulted in mixing and integration. Indeed, the texts usually express the Egyptian royal ideology centred on the opposition between cosmic order and chaotic forces and emphasize the role of the ruler as the controller of the potentially chaotic foreigners, while the foreigners are usually presented as invariably vanquished and submissive. Yet the reality was that the different groups were living side by side, interacting and integrating in several contexts.

The aforementioned Nubian soldiers who had been serving in Egypt at least since the late Old Kingdom may have been well integrated into Egyptian society (Sections 2.2, 3.1). A group of stelae from the region of Gebelein in Upper Egypt dating to the First Intermediate Period can be ascribed to some of these soldiers (Ejsmond 2019; Fischer 1961; Seidlmayer 2002: 100–1). These men can be identified as Nubians not only because they often call themselves Nubians, but also because their attire and attributes are typical of Nubian soldiers, such as a bag or perhaps an animal tail hanging from their belt and the presence of a bow, which is a typical Nubian weapon (Figure 19). In addition, they are also accompanied by their dogs, not because these were the family pets, but because these are further attributes that refer to their role of warriors. As they are often depicted accompanying the soldiers, perhaps when patrolling the desert, the dogs were, like the bow, indeed part of their equipment. Although stressing their Nubian identity, and proudly presenting themselves as warriors, these men are at the same time expressing their successful integration into Egyptian society: the stelae feature Egyptian hieroglyphic inscriptions with the usual offering formula, and the structure of the iconographic composition is typical of this period and shows the family of the soldier, including the wife sometimes depicted nearby the husband. Unfortunately, few data are available on the funerary monuments upon which these stelae were placed, but we can expect that they were associating Egyptian and Nubian features, as was possibly the case for other tombs at Gebelein as well (Ejsmond 2019: 28–31). Moreover, there the Nubians were apparently buried at the same cemetery as the Egyptians. Thus, all these remarks suggest that there were Nubians proud of their origin but who were still perfectly integrated into Egyptian society. The fact that they could afford to build or were given such a kind of funerary monuments also suggests that they had reached a good level of social and economic success. It should be stressed that most likely this was not the first case of foreigners that had successfully integrated into Egyptian society. A further case may perhaps be found in the Archaic cemetery of Helwan, where a stele was found that represents a foreigner, which according to his hair-dress may be a Puntite or a Nubian (Fischer 1963: 34–9). This case is similar to the ones of the stelae from Gebelein, as the fact that a complex funerary monument was available to this foreigner demonstrates that he had not only integrated into Egyptian society, but also that he had also reached quite a high social status.

But the socio-cultural integration may have followed different paths and reached different degrees, consequently resulting in different material expressions. Remaining in Upper Egypt, but in the later phases of the Middle Kingdom and Second Intermediate Period, important data on the Nubian presence have been recorded at Hierakonpolis. Three distinct Nubian

cemeteries, which were spatially separated from each other and from the
Egyptian cemetery, with clear differences in terms of material culture and
funerary habits, were recorded at the site: two Pan-Grave burial areas date to
the Second Intermediate Period, while the C-Group cemetery is earlier and
dates to the Eleventh to Twelfth Dynasties (Friedman 2001). In particular,
despite the close dating, the C-Group cemetery contrasts with the case of the
Egyptian monuments most likely associated with the stelae of the aforementioned First Intermediate Period Nubian soldiers, in that no inscriptions occur.
Furthermore, the funerary superstructures – round tumuli – and the funerary
rituals are typically Nubian (Figure 24). Of course, adaptations to the local
milieu can be observed: at Hierakonpolis the tumuli sometimes have their
foundations made with mud bricks rather than with stones. It is difficult to
explain why in the case of the C-Group cemetery at Hierakonpolis the will to
maintain and to stress identity is so marked when compared to the stelae of
the Nubian soldiers. This emphasis on identity may merely be a matter of
more recent integration of these groups into the Egyptian socio-cultural
setting. Nevertheless, the possibility that other factors may have somehow
limited integration cannot be excluded, like perhaps in the case of the Pepy I's
decree from Dashur forbidding Nubians not only from carrying out any
requisitions but also from becoming priests in the pyramid towns
(Seidlmayer 2002: 97). Anyway, the integration of these groups into the
Egyptian socio-economic setting is evident at Hierakonpolis as Egyptian
vessels are found among the grave goods in the C-Group cemetery (Giuliani
2001: 40). These Egyptian vessels were closed jars and were most likely used
as transport and/or storage containers for various commodities and supplies.
In contrast, Nubian pottery is mostly represented by open forms for food
preparation and consumption. The fact that Egyptian vessels were used for
transport and/or storage and Nubian pottery for serving and cooking suggests
that these groups may have been integrated into local economy, possibly even
into the redistributive system of the Egyptian state. A similar pattern in terms
of composition of the ceramic assemblage can also be observed in the Pan-
Grave cemeteries of the late Twelfth Dynasty to the Second Intermediate
Period. These burial grounds are located across a wide area from Middle
Egypt to Lower Nubia, and are moreover marked by an increasing incorporation of Egyptian elements in the later assemblages, even though typical Pan-
Grave traits remain dominant (de Souza 2020: 3–4). Was this incorporation
related to an increasing socio-economic integration of those groups, to
a growing openness to Egyptian culture or perhaps both? Indeed, similar
dynamics are also known during later times. A Blemmyan community flour-
ished in Gebelein in the sixth century AD and the fact that the names of its

**Figure 24** View of the HK27C C-Group cemetery at Hierakonpolis dating to the Eleventh to Twelfth Dynasties (Photographer James Rossiter © Hierakonpolis Expedition).

members also occur on legal documents related to the management of properties confirms that some of these Blemmyans had a certain level of affluence (Eide et al.1998: 1196–216). Their presence in the Egyptian Nile valley may be explained by the fact that the Egyptian Byzantine administration allowed them to settle there because they were 'federates' (i.e. allies), yet at the same time they appeared to have retained their own social and political structure, despite the fact that they were using Greek and Coptic for their legal documents and that some of them may have adopted Christianity, as shown by their names.

Since the earliest phases, Egyptians and Africans were also living side by side in areas outside Egypt. This can be seen when the Egyptian state established outposts and fortresses to control specific parts of the neighbouring regions. The Nubian ceramics from the Old Kingdom settlement at Buhen (Section 2.2) suggest that some Nubians may have interacted with the Egyptians settled there and were perhaps even living among them (O'Connor 2014: 304). Archaeological evidence from the Middle to New Kingdom demonstrates that the occupants of the Egyptian fortresses in Lower Nubia were interacting with the inhabitants of the region, some of them possibly also living inside the Egyptian settlements (Smith 2003: 133–5). In particular, detailed examination of the Middle Kingdom phases at Askut has shown that when Egyptian expatriate communities sprang up in the fortresses, a substantial frequency of Nubian cooking vessels began to characterize the ceramic assemblages. These cooking vessels were interpreted as evidence of Nubian women being in charge of cooking and as a possible evidence of intermarriage with Egyptian men. Similar situations may also have characterized Egyptian settlements in Nubia in New Kingdoms times (Section 2.3). Attestation of this was found at Tombos in the cemetery of an Egyptian administrative centre in the Third Cataract region. This cemetery showed that structures and funerary rituals that were both typically Egyptian and Nubian coexisted side by side (Smith 2003: 136–66). Furthermore, the Nubian traits, which are on the whole in a much lower quantity when compared to the Egyptian elements, are often associated with women. This again suggests that the integration between the two communities may have included intermarriage. As far as the Nubian sites dating to the period of the Egyptian Middle Kingdom occupation of Lower Nubia are concerned, these settlements echo the case of the Nubian cemeteries in Hierakonpolis. Cultural integration of Nubians into the predominantly Egyptian socio-cultural context finds support in the presence of Egyptian materials among their grave goods and the presence of Egyptian closed jars highlights that the Nubians were somehow involved in the Egyptian economic system (Hasfaas 2005: 86–7, 141).

It goes without saying that in these cases foreigners did not hold an equal position in the dynamics of interaction. Nevertheless, despite starting out from such a disadvantage, these foreigners were still able to reach important positions in society, as the First Intermediate Period funerary stelae of Nubian soldiers from Upper Egypt suggest. Perhaps one of the most successful cases of the integration of foreigners into Egyptian socio-cultural contexts is represented by the Libyan communities in Egypt, which were most likely formed with the consent of the Egyptian state at the end of the New Kingdom. This took place when some of these Libyans were integrated into the Egyptian army, which after some generations and intermarriage with the Egyptian elite led to the rise of the Libyan dynasties ruling over Egypt (Morkot 2016a: 33). At the beginning of the first millennium BC, Nubian officials who arrived in Egypt after the conquest of the country by the Nubian rulers of the Twenty-Fifth Dynasty (Section 2.4) were also able to maintain important positions in the Theban region even after the Assyrians put an end to Nubian rule and the rise of the Twenty-Sixth Dynasty (Morkot 2000: 299–301). A high social rank often characterized the foreigners settling in Egypt in the framework of diplomatic interactions (Section 3.1). The fact that some of princesses, who came from the regions south of Egypt, may have reached a very high status in the Egyptian court may be supported by the Nubian origin suggested for some of the royal ladies buried in the temple of Mentuhotep II at Deir el-Bahari (Ejsmond 2019: 36; Morkot 2000: 52–3).

Nevertheless, although their Nubian origin remains a possibility, it cannot be proven, and the issue remains highly debated. Moreover, it is also possible, but not indisputably proven, that the mother of the Hyksos king named Nehesi ('the Nubian') may have been a Nubian woman (Ryholt 2018: 268–9). Perhaps, she herself was the offspring of a well-connected Nubian family resident in Egypt, or even a princess who had arrived at Avaris as part of diplomatic exchanges between the Hyksos and the Kushites in the Second Intermediate Period (Sections 2.3, 3.1). Such a kind of relations may have also involved Thebes, as suggested by a tantalizing Seventeenth Dynasty tomb of an unfortunately anonymous woman and a child possibly linked to the royal family, containing six Kerma beakers (Roehrig 2005: 15–16, 21–2). Leaving aside the controversial Nubian origin or the Nubian connections of some members of the royal family, we know that the system of deporting Nubian elite offspring as hostages may have resulted not only in their Egyptian education, but also in their integration into the upper echelons of Egyptian society (Section 2.3). A good example is perhaps represented by Maiherperi, a Nubian educated in the Kap, the institution in the royal court where the royal princes were also educated (Roehrig 2005: 70; Morkot 2000: 85). Although unfortunately very little is known about him, the influence he was able to acquire in the court is indeed evident by the great honour he was given, as he was buried in the Valley of the Kings, the final resting place of the Egyptian rulers of the New Kingdom (Morkot 2013: 948). In sum, this points to foreigners from the other African regions being able to successfully integrate into Egyptian society, and eventually achieving an important social status. This was most likely possible throughout all the phases of Egyptian history, although certainly the conditions allowing such integration may have been more or less favourable according to the social and historical circumstances of each individual period.

Although we do not have an equivalent of the Tale of Sinuhe set in an African region, namely a tale describing the ability of an Egyptian expatriate to successfully integrate into a foreign context and reach a high status, similar cases may also have taken place in Nubia. Some evidence is available for the Second Intermediate Period, when the kingdom of Kush was able to extend its sphere of influence north of the Second Cataract and to establish its control over the fortresses built by the Egyptian Twelfth Dynasty rulers (Section 2.2). As mentioned, expatriate Egyptian communities developed in Lower Nubia and continued to remain there after the end of Egyptian state control of the region. When hegemony in Lower Nubia passed to the kingdom of Kush, some members of the Egyptian families living in the fortresses, which had already provided officials to the Egyptian administration, were serving the king of Kush. This clearly emerges from some of the stelae from the fortress of

Buhen (Török 2009: 106–8). In particular, Sopedhor, a member of a local Egyptian family, built a temple dedicated to the Horus of Buhen for the king of Kush, while Ka, also a member of a local Egyptian family, travelled to Kush, perhaps to carry out activities related to rituals, which also involved the Nubian king (Figure 25). Perhaps similar situations also took place at the end of the New Kingdom, when the Egyptian control of Nubia ended and Egyptian expatriates may have started serving the fledgling Nubian polities from which sprang the Twenty-Fifth Dynasty, but unfortunately this phase remains largely obscure (Morkot 2000: 133; Török 1997: 111, 120–1).

Indeed, from at least the New Kingdom onwards, an important group of Egyptian temporary or permanent expatriates may have been represented by priests, who were settling in the Egyptian administrative centres located in Nubia, which always had one or more temples. The role of the institutions in which they were serving was certainly not only religious, but also economic in nature (Section 2.3). It is reasonable to suggest that the presence of this kind of individuals also continued after the end of Egyptian control over Nubia (Török 2002: 16, 49) and that they had successfully integrated into Nubian society. At that time, the close relations between the Amun temple at Karnak and the clergy of its southern counterpart at Jebel Barkal may have been crucial not only from a cultural and ideological perspective (Török 2002: 51–4; see Section 3.3), but also in terms of favouring the political and military involvement of the Nubian kings in Egypt in the mid-eighth century BC (Sections 2.4, 3.3). That such kinds of presences were continuing in Meroitic times can be seen by some of the texts in the Temple of the Lion at Musawwarat es-Sufra. Indeed, these texts may have been inspired by some texts in the temple of Isis at Philae (Török 1997: 502). They suggest that contacts between the clergies at the two ceremonial centres took place, perhaps involving the presence of Egyptian priests in Nubian sanctuaries and vice-versa, which fits well with the framework of the diplomatic relations between the Meroitic kingdom and Ptolemaic and Roman Egypt, in which the role of Philae was crucial (Sections 2.5, 3.1). The process of priests leaving Egypt for its African neighbours and successfully integrating into local society continued up until Christian times, which is mainly known to us from textual sources (Section 2.6). However, some contemporary epigraphic data, such as the large number of graffiti inscriptions in Coptic in Nubian monasteries also serve to highlight this process and may suggest presences of Egyptian monks in these Nubian communities (Welsby 2002: 238). As far as the more southern regions are concerned, in the Ethio-Eritrean highlands the patriarch of the local church in Aksumite and Medieval times may have been an Egyptian or at least a foreigner appointed to the position by the patriarch of

**Figure 25** The Second Intermediate Period stela of Ka from Buhen
(Photographer Rocco Ricci © The British Museum).

Alexandria, as was the case in later periods. Nevertheless, it should be stressed that for the earliest phases the evidence that this procedure was already in place is debated (Phillipson 2012: 87–8).

Finally, the establishment in foreign lands of small groups of people and their successful integration into local society may also have been due to trade activities. Nevertheless, unfortunately these dynamics often remain obscure, given the scarce attention paid to private traders and trade in the texts and the difficulty to reconstruct them on archaeological grounds. A community of foreign traders was likely settled at Adulis, the Aksumite port on the Red Sea, in the first century AD, as suggested in *Periplus of the Erythrean Sea*. In this context too, it remains feasible that some expatriates were able to integrate into local society and to reach a high level of affluence. This possibility is high-lighted by the story of Frumentius. Although not originally from Egypt but from Tyrus, and not even a member of the resident community of traders but a traveller seized by pirates on the Eritrean coast, Frumentius was able to achieve a very important role in the Aksumite court, together with his compan-ion Aedesius, being crucial in the process of adoption of Christianity by the king. Subsequently, he was also appointed first patriarch of the Ethiopian church by Athanasius of Alexandria in the first half of the fourth century AD (Phillipson 2012: 91–3).

## 3.3 Cultural Encounters, Entanglements and Selective Adoptions

A series of cultural dynamics were taking place within the framework of the various interactions between Egypt and its African neighbours, which included the movements of single individuals or larger groups as well as the formation of expatriate communities (Sections 3.1, 3.2). These dynamics led to the adoption of foreign cultural elements and traits as well as to processes of cultural entanglement between diverse groups. Of course, such foreign traits often gained new meanings and functions different from those they held in their original contexts. These dynamics are mostly visible in the archaeological remains, but in a few cases textual sources can also provide us with important information on them. As far as archaeology is concerned, such dynamics can be detected across a variety of different contexts, from single objects, to whole assemblages, from everyday objects, to the artworks and high-quality artifacts related to the elite milieu.

As early as the fifth millennium BC, the sharing of several material culture traits is found in the funerary assemblages of a broad area, including Upper Egypt and several upstream regions of the Nile valley. This distribution of traits could support the hypothesis that cultural contact and interaction between those regions was occurring (Section 2.1). On this basis, it was also suggested that similar ritual practices were adopted in the different regions of the Nile valley (Wengrow et al. 2014: 107), although of course, the meaning given to the shared elements could have varied from context to context. The fact that the elements related to this shared horizon appear at an earlier date in the Middle Nile area when compared to Upper Egypt, prompts the idea that in this specific phase the cultural traits originating in the southern regions were adopted in the latter (Wengrow et al. 2014: 102, 105). The presumption that the southern areas, especially the Sudanese Nile valley, were exclusively pastoral in terms of their economic base has been recently questioned (Salvatori & Usai 2019: 272–4). Yet several of the elements characterizing this funerary horizon, such as the cattle skulls that were perhaps related to ritual funerary meals (Figure 6), can certainly be regarded as traces of the social and perhaps ideological importance that the control of cattle had for those groups (Wengrow et al. 2014: 105–6). Such symbolism related to cattle is also well evident in the inland areas, away from the Nile valley, where a predominantly pastoral adaptive system may have been more widely adopted. The finds in the hinterland areas include a fifth millennium BC ritual burial of cattle at Nabta Playa in the Western Desert (Wendorf & Schild 2002: 17). It may be precisely from those contexts that these cultural traits were spreading to the Nile valley including Egypt, especially if the intense relations between the valley and inland areas in that phase are also taken into account (Section 2.1). The cultural and ideological links between Egyptian culture and this cattle pastoral ideological horizon, which also characterized its African neighbours, are possibly reflected in predynastic and dynastic art, which often allude to the symbolic role of cattle (Wendorf & Schild 2002: 19). For example, in the well-known Narmer palette, not only are the heads of a cow deity symmetrically arranged on the upper side of the object, but the king himself is represented as a mighty bull slaying his enemies (Smith 2018: 336).

In addition to that, some of the ceremonial structures brought to light in Nabta Playa may have had an astronomical function (Wendorf & Schild 2002: 17). Therefore, it was suggested that ideas originating in the Nile valley hinterland were even contributing to the rise of Egyptian astronomical knowledge, although of course this hypothesis remains largely unproven. A further element suggesting the contribution of the regions west and east of the Nile valley to the rise of Egyptian culture is the similarity between some of the rock art scenes in the desert regions and iconographies of predynastic and dynastic art (Bárta 2018: 672, 675–9). Of course, uncertainties remain on this evidence due to the debatable chronology of the rock art (Smith 2018: 331–2). Nevertheless, the emergence of concepts perhaps related to the cosmic order and its affirmation – a crucial issue in Egyptian kingship up until the end of the pharaonic history – might lie behind representations like those of captured or killed wild animals or enemies, which occur in the desert rock art. Therefore, this is potentially a further contribution of the regions east and west of the Nile valley to the ideological aspects of Egyptian culture (Bárta 2018: 681–3; Darnell 2007: 33). Of course, along with the elements related to the ideological sphere, in the sixth and fifth millennia BC, technologies were also shared, as is evident from the similarities in the lithic and ceramic industries between Egypt and its neighbours remarked upon in Section 2.1.

Such dynamics did not come to an end after the emergence of the Egyptian dynastic culture. With regard to later phases, interesting examples of cultural entanglements have recently been pointed out in aspects of material culture that are more related to everyday life. A good example was identified through an examination of Egyptian ceramic production at the end of the First Intermediate Period and early Middle Kingdom (Rzeuska 2010). At the end of the third millennium BC, Upper Egyptian ceramics feature incised, impressed and moulded decorations, whose appearance is somehow surprising when considering that the decorations generally disappeared from Egyptian pottery at the end of the fourth millennium BC. It has been observed that some of the decorative patterns now found on Upper Egyptian pottery are similar to those on Lower Nubian ceramics, and it cannot be excluded that some of these patterns refer to more southern ceramic traditions, such as the one of Eastern Sudan (Manzo 2020a: 10–11). This is certainly not surprising as the adoption of southern traits by Upper Egyptian potters is likely to have taken place as a consequence of contacts with southern regions, which are well known for that phase (Section 2.2). Certainly, these dynamics found favourable conditions in the specific location of Upper Egypt, which was particularly conducive to contacts with the southern regions. Moreover, it is well known that at that time communities of Nubians were living in Upper Egypt (Sections 3.1, 3.2). Nevertheless, the crucial point is to address the issue of why these southern cultural traits were adopted, because mere exposure to another culture does not automatically lead to its adoption nor even of adoption of some of its elements. Indeed, as the iconographic and textual sources suggest, some aspects of the southern cultures may have been appreciated in Egypt at that time.

Roughly in the same phase entanglement between the ceramic tradition of the Nubians settled in Egypt and the Egyptian ceramic traditions took place as well. Some of the vessels from the Nubian cemeteries in Egypt (Sections 3.1, 3.2) reveal some insights into this process. Among these is an Egyptian cup from the C-Group cemetery at Hierakonpolis (Figure 26). It can be ascribed to a well-known Egyptian type, but it is characterized by a blackened effect on the inside and around the rim. The intention was clearly to make the cup look like a Nubian black-topped vessel (Giuliani 2001: 40) and a similar practice has also been highlighted at Mersa/Wadi Gawasis, another site characterized by the presence of Nubian materials (Manzo 2010: 443; Section 3.1). Thus, in those cases, Egyptian objects were Nubianized by Nubian residents in Egypt most likely because of the specific role the black-topped vessels had in the Nubian cultural milieu, especially with regard to funerary ceremonies and in general the consumption of food and drink. As far as ceramics are concerned, we can find traces of entanglement in other Nubian cultures as well. The Pan-Grave culture

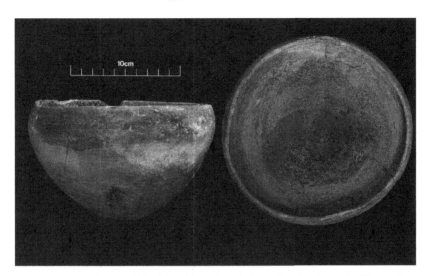

**Figure 26** Egyptian cup blackened inside and along the rim from the Eleventh to Twelfth Dynasties C Group HK27C cemetery at Hierakonpolis (Photographer James Rossiter © Hierakonpolis Expedition).

has a series of vessels that feature traits deriving from the Egyptian ceramic repertoire, and some vessels characterized by Pan-Grave appearance were made through the use of Egyptian technology (de Souza 2020: 8–14). Similarly, Upper Nubian Kerma pottery shows signs of imitation of Egyptian ceramic vessels from the end of the third millennium BC onwards (see Gratien 1978: 175, 208). In this case, the imitations were mainly closed bottles, which reproduced the classes of vessels imported from Egypt, most likely as containers for commodities. The imitation of the containers is possibly related to the highly appreciated and much-desired status such imported commodities held in Nubian contexts, where access to such kinds of goods was likely also connected to the display of high social rank.

Such phenomena widely occurred in the relations between Egypt and its African neighbours throughout the centuries. However, as stressed earlier, they only took place in favourable cultural conditions. Remaining in the field of ceramic studies, it is well known that Meroitic painted pottery, dating from the end of the first millennium BC to the beginning of the first millennium AD, was probably influenced, and perhaps even ultimately inspired, by Hellenistic painted ceramics (Török 2011: 239–300). In addition, the shape of some Meroitic vessels was certainly inspired by Roman fine wares and/or by highly prized metal vessels of Mediterranean production, which were also imported into the Meroitic kingdom (Manzo 2013). Further south, imitations of Mediterranean amphorae, fine wares and possibly imported metal- and glassware have also been identified in Aksumite ceramics of the first half of the first millennium AD (Manzo 2003). Similar to the case of the earlier imitation of Egyptian ceramics in Upper Nubia, the reason that some Meroitic and Aksumite ceramics were inspired by Mediterranean prototypes may lay in the fact that Mediterranean imports were highly sought-after goods and their availability was most likely limited to the elite. This exclusive status transformed the imported vessels into rank markers, which in turn led to their imitation by local potters. In both the Meroitic and Aksumite contexts this was certainly taking place within a framework of interactions where the adoption of foreign cultural traits of Mediterranean origin was occurring (Török 2011), not only as far as aspects of material culture are concerned, but possibly also in terms of lifestyles. Indeed, the wide distribution of Mediterranean wine amphorae and vessels related to wine consumption in Meroitic elite contexts may be evidence of the adoption of wine and its accompanying paraphernalia (Manzo 2006: 84).

In the meantime, Mediterranean ideological traits associated with wine are also visible in the Meroitic art of the period and are especially linked to Apedemak, a local lion-headed deity. References to Apedemak occur in contexts where representations related to the Dionysiac Mediterranean wine-cult abound, such as the Water Sanctuary in Meroe and the façades of the palace of King Natakamani in Jebel Barkal (Manzo 2006). Other examples of the adoption of iconographic motifs from the north are known in Meroitic context, such as the case of the representations of solar and fertility deities, which can be related to Helios and Serapis in the Lion Temple at Naga (Török 2011: 321–2). The most famous example is perhaps the rock carved triumphal scene at Jebel Queili, where a deity with solar and fertility attributes is represented facing a much more traditional representation of King Shorkarhor (Hintze 1959) (Figure 27). Indeed, from the third century BC, several iconographic traits on Meroitic monuments and perhaps even their possible ideological meanings bear some relation to Ptolemaic Egypt (Török 2002: 193–200). In general, as far as the Hellenistic Mediterranean elements are concerned, it should be remarked that their adoption may express the political ambitions of the Meroitic elite, thereby adhering to practices shared with the other aristocracies of the time and ultimately largely rooted in the imperial ideology set by Alexander the Great and continued in Egypt by the Ptolemies.

Indisputably, the most evident adoption of exogenous cultural elements is visible in the monuments produced under the patronage of the Nubian rulers in the early first millennium BC. At that time, the Nubian rulers of the Twenty-Fifth Dynasty presented themselves as legitimate heirs to Egyptian kingship and the Egyptian dynastic tradition (Section 2.4). This is well expressed in the victory stela of Pye that commemorates the Nubians gaining control over Egypt. This

**Figure 27** Solar deity of Hellenistic type with the first century AD Meroitic king
Shorkarhor at Jebel Queili (from *Kush* 7, courtesy National Corporation for
Antiquities and Museums).

stele finds its inspiration in the triumphal stelae of New Kingdom period, or to be more precise, in the ones erected at Jebel Barkal. Both the structure and composition of the text show similarities to the New Kingdom royal inscriptions, just as the other Twenty-Fifth Dynasty and Napatan texts do (Eide et al. 1994: 62–118). Moreover, in the text Pye presents himself as the keeper of Egyptian tradition. This was a lasting approach: for generations the Nubian rulers bore the title of king of Upper and Lower Egypt even after the end of their control over Egypt. Despite the intense ties Middle Nile elites established with Egypt in the New Kingdom (Sections 2.3, 3.2), this alone does not explain the deep Egyptian impact on the Nubian kingship during the early first millennium BC. Noteworthy is that Egyptian traits are not very visible in the earliest tombs found in the El-Kurru cemetery, where Pye, his ancestors and his immediate successors were buried, yet a process of adoption of elements from Egyptian funerary rituals can be reconstructed (Török 1997: 115–23). Therefore, in this case, we can suggest that the adoption of features of Egyptian funerary religion and more generally culture was a deliberate act. This was possibly directly related to the political ambitions of the rulers buried at El-Kurru. They first established their control over the various parts of Nubia, where at different degrees some Egyptian cultural elements were already adopted, and from a certain point onwards began extending it over Egypt itself, where they were recognized as legitimate rulers. Indeed, all this may be reflected in the progressive Egyptianization of their funerary rituals. The attention paid to the Egyptian traditions is shown in this specific phase also by the rediscovery and philological re-use of artistic styles and iconographies dating back mainly to Old and Middle Kingdom times. A good example of this is the scene representing Taharka as a sphinx trampling the Libyan enemies in the temple he built at Kawa, which faithfully reproduces earlier scenes from the funerary complexes of the rulers of the Fifth and Sixth Dynasties (Török 2002: 93–4) (Figure 28). It should be stressed that a similar use of traits originating from earlier phases of the Egyptian royal iconography and titulary is not unique in the first millennium BC, as it also characterizes the Libyan dynasties in Egypt (Morkot 2007: 145–8).

Although the Egyptian impact may appear dominant and exclusive in Twenty-Fifth Dynasty artworks, some elements show how exogenous traits were re-worked into a wholly Nubian socio-cultural framework. Remaining in the royal milieu, this reworking of Egyptian culture into Nubian contexts emerges from the insistence on the presence of royal ladies, queens and princesses on royal monuments. They are frequently depicted accompanying the ruler while acting in their role as priestesses in the scenes where the king is performing his legitimizing interaction with the gods. Furthermore, on the stela of King Aspleta, dating to the very beginning of the sixth century BC, a long line

**Figure 28** The Twenty-Fifth Dynasty king Taharka represented as a sphinx trampling over his Libyan enemies in the temple he built in Kawa (from Macadam 1949).

of female ancestors are listed to legitimate the royal ascent to the throne, which is certainly unusual from a purely Egyptian perspective (Eide et al. 1994: 232–52). Moreover, long before Pye and perhaps dating to the very beginning of the first millennium BC, one of the earliest documents to refer to the control of a Nubian dynasty over Lower Nubia is the inscription of Queen Katimala carved on the façade of the temple of Semna. This inscription is closely related to contemporary Egyptian iconography, palaeography and language, but it was dedicated by a queen, not a king, and although a reference to a king, perhaps her husband, is present in the text, his name is not mentioned (Darnell 2006: 55–63). All of these elements suggest that female members of the Nubian royal family had crucial political and dynastic roles, which can be regarded as a Nubian trait. The reason for this is that in some contexts in north-eastern Africa to the south of Egypt women traditionally had great importance in social terms, and this is a feature that clearly emerges in the later Meroitic phase, but is already evident in Twenty-Fifth Dynasty and Napatan times (Lowhasser 2001). Going back to artworks, in the case of the royal monuments of the Libyan dynasties ruling over Egypt at the beginning of the first millennium BC, similar processes can be outlined. For example, some distinctive Libyan feather headdresses are some-times associated with typically Egyptian royal attributes (Morkot 2007: 147).

The Twenty-Fifth Dynasty period was not the first time that traits related to Egyptian kingship were adopted by Nubian rulers. A further example is found at the very end of the fourth to early third millennium BC in the earliest expressions of Nubian kingship, which were discovered in the A-Group Cemetery L at Qustul. This is a burial ground whose tombs are exceptional for the quality and quantity of grave goods (Williams 1986: 163). Several objects from the tombs feature iconographies closely related to those on the artworks of the first Egyptian rulers (Williams 1986: 182–3), whose earliest examples pre-date the finds from Qustul L (Gatto 2006: 66; Török 2009: 42–3). A very good example of this is seen in one of the incense burners, where a person wearing a crown certainly reminiscent of the Egyptian white crown is depicted along with a line of boats (Figure 2). Other elements in the scene incorporate more local aspects, such as the palace façade pattern, which has a very typical and distinctive shape, different from the one of the Egyptian *serekh* (Williams 1986: 143–4). This may suggest that at that time some symbols and patterns related to kingship of an Egyptian origin were adopted by Nubian rulers, although their aspect was sometimes modified. Their meaning in the Nubian context is also likely to have differed at least partially from the significance they held in the context where they originated. Noteworthy, similar processes were noticed in contexts related to the kingship of the kingdom of Kush, such as the monumental buildings at Kerma.

Although these buildings are very distinctive and typically local, their southern façades were sometimes characterized by pylon-like structures and their lintels were sometimes decorated by winged sun disks, like the temples built by the kings of Egypt (Bonnet 2000: 100, 126, 128; 2004: 45).

If only these cases are considered, one may get the impression that this was an overwhelming one-way process, in which the southern side was always adopting traits from the north, of course reworking the adopted elements in order to pursue specific purposes and express typically local messages. On the contrary, similar dynamics were probably at work in Egypt, with the adoption into the elite milieu of specific traits originating from, or at least related to, the southern regions. Some tombs at Meir in Middle Egypt can be ascribed to the local nomarchs going back to the early Twelfth Dynasty. Represented in one of these tombs are scenes of the hunt in the desert and among the figures is a man wearing Nubian or perhaps Libyan attire (Moreno García 2018: 163) while hunting. It was suggested that he was an Egyptian aristocrat (Fischer 1961: 74), perhaps the son of the owner of the tomb according to Blackman (1914: 31), although this has recently been questioned by Kanawati (2017: 271, n. 37). Be that as it may, the adoption of foreign attire may be related to the fact that Nubians and Libyans were highly appreciated in Egypt as hunters and warriors (Ejsmond 2019: 27–8, 34; Sections 2.2, 3.2), as both war and hunting were closely linked activities in Egypt, just as they were elsewhere. The appreciation for these skills possessed by the Nubians also continued in later times. This is perhaps visible in the fact that fly pendants, the awards symbolizing military valour in Egypt from the very end of the Seventeenth Dynasty to the mid-Eighteenth Dynasty, were probably inspired by similar pendants found in earlier tombs at Kerma (Binder 2008: 49–55), where they may already have had a similar meaning (Manzo 2016: 24). Further evidence from the early New Kingdom, which was a phase of widening horizons for Egyptian culture, also includes the adoption of other kinds of personal ornaments of possible African origin. This may be the case of earrings, which may have been adopted in the Egyptian elite milieu in the early Eighteenth Dynasty (Andrews 1990: 111; see also Morkot 2007: 147–8). Perhaps not by chance, one of the earliest pieces of evidence of use of earrings from the milieu of the Egyptian court was detected on the mummy of the aforementioned aristocrat of Nubian origin Maiherperi (Roehrig 2005: 70; Section 3.2).

Indeed, after the establishment of Egyptian hegemony over the Middle Nile valley in the early New Kingdom, several Nubian traits are also likely to have been re-worked into the sphere of Egyptian kingship and religion. This is surprising when considering the absolute ideological rejection of all that was foreign that usually emerges from the royal texts (Section 1.3). The monument that most explicitly marks the Egyptian act of taking control of the southern regions is the boundary stela by Thutmosis I, carved on a granite hill at Hagar el-Merwa, between the Fourth and the Fifth Cataracts, which was later on duplicated by Thutmosis III after his Nubian campaigns (Davies 2017; Section 2.3). The text is accompanied by a representation of the royal name in front of the god Amun, which is scarcely surprising when considering the centrality of Amun in the Egyptian pantheon of that period and his intimate links with kingship. What is interesting, however, is the fact that we have on this stela one of the earliest representations of the ram-headed Amun (Davies 2017: 69) (Figure 29). Yet, the choice of this innovative iconography on a royal monument was certainly deliberate and may be explained by its Nubian context. Indeed, the fact that rams were considered to be sacred animals is well evident at Kerma (Kendall 1997: 76–8). Among other things it should be stressed that a statue of a ram-headed lion, which may be the earliest criosphinx found in the whole Nile valley so far, was discovered in tumulus K III, certainly a royal funerary monument of a king of Kush (Bonnet 2004: 158). Therefore, among the Egyptian iconographic representations to which elements from neighbour African regions may have contributed are the ram-headed Amun and the criosphinx, destined to became crucial divine iconographies in Egypt itself.

Returning to the Hagar el-Merwa boundary stelae, these stelae are also associated with two inscriptions mentioning the 'Amun-ra bull of his mother'. The hieroglyph sign representing the bull in the inscriptions is deliberately oversized, of course representing the deity himself (Davies 2017: 69), but also serves to somehow provide a sense of continuity between the inscription and the earlier representations of cattle that were likely left on the same rock by local pastoral groups prior to the arrival of the army of Thutmosis I (Figure 30). Therefore, in this case as well, we may detect the deliberate use of symbols referring to the Nubian cultural milieu on an Egyptian royal monument. Perhaps the aim was to express Egyptian hegemony over the area through the use of an iconographic and ideological language that could be understood in the local cultural context. Furthermore, by doing this at Hagar el-Merwa, the Egyptians also appropriated a place that, as suggested by the local rock art characterizing the site, may have been regarded as a land marker by the inhabitants of the region: the aim was arguably to tie the iconographic language to the physical landscape (Davies 2017: 94). Finally, the two painted striding lions at Hagar el-Merwa should also be considered part of this trend (Davies 2017: 69) (Figure 31). The choice of a lion representation should not be a surprise as in Egypt the lion was a royal symbol from at least the late fourth millennium BC. Nevertheless, it may not be a coincidence that in this specific case the

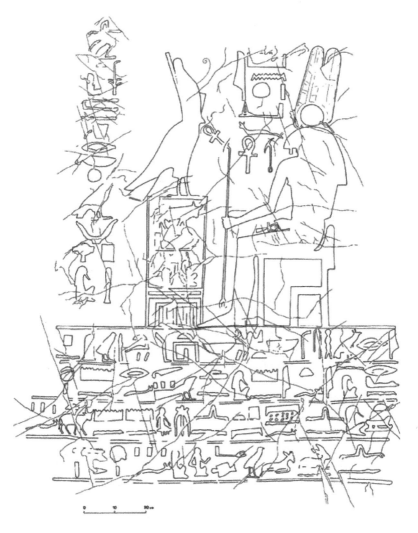

**Figure 29** Ram-headed Amun facing the royal name in the boundary stela of Thutmosis I at Hajar el-Merowa (courtesy Vivian Davies).

iconography chosen to represent the lion has clear affinities to the lions used on the façade of chapel K II at Kerma, a royal funerary monument of a king of Kush (Kendall 1997: 72). The distinctive and similar iconography of a sign on a rock inscription in the Eastern Desert of Nubia, which may represent a title or an epithet in association with the name of a king of Kush (Davies 2014: 35–6) may not be casual (Figure 5). Moreover, in Eighteenth Dynasty Egypt, pendants representing striding lions were sometimes associated with the aforementioned fly awards perhaps inspired by Nubian prototypes (Binder 2008: 55–7). This

**Figure 30** Inscriptions of Thutmosis I and Thutmosis III mentioning Amun-ra 'Bull of his mother', associated with earlier Nubian pastoral rock art at Hajar el-Merowa (courtesy Vivian Davies).

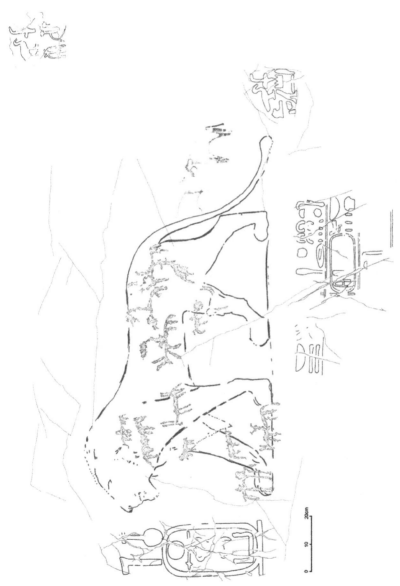

**Figure 31** The striding lion of Thutmosis I at Hajar el-Merowa (courtesy Vivian Davies).

may be a further case of intentional use of a trait from the southern regions in the Egyptian context.

These are certainly not the only contributions to Egyptian ideological and religious tradition originating in its African neighbours for dynastic times. Further examples can be found, sometimes in unexpected contexts, as for some Meroitic epithets and names in some spells of the Book of the Dead (Rilly 2007: 11–14). Therefore, these last examples confirm that, in the long history of interactions between Egypt and its African neighbours, adoption, adaptation and entanglement can be detected on both sides.

## 4 Conclusions

This Element had the ambition to provide some insights into the issue of the relations between Egypt and its African neighbours. After summarizing the history of scholarship on the topic and how its perspective has changed, the environmental setting in which the relations took place was discussed, and a summary of the history of the relations outlined. We ended our review with a discussion of the modes of interaction between Egypt and its African neighbours and their socio-cultural effects. Naturally, only some of the many possible cases were explored in the final section and this is due to space constraints. Nevertheless, I hope that the need to put Egypt back into its African setting emerged from this discussion. The recontextualization of Egypt into its African setting is important not only for Egyptology, but also for African history and archaeology as a whole. The study of this issue also offers much potential for the general anthropological debate on cultural exchanges and interactions and on relevant anthropological concepts, such as entanglement. I also hope to have highlighted the fact that debate on several specific issues is still ongoing as well as the fact that intense scholarly work is needed to fully explore some of them, while new themes are also emerging.

Indeed, the study of the relations between Egypt and its African neighbours is still biased by the limited knowledge we currently have of some of the areas involved, which is largely due to limited archaeological fieldwork. While a lot has been achieved in the Middle Nile valley, the limits of our present knowledge are still quite evident for other African regions around Egypt. For example, in the case of the northern Libyan desert, where some important groups who greatly determined the historical trajectory of Egypt suddenly emerged at the end of the second millennium BC (Sections 2.3, 3.1), almost nothing is known of the local peoples for the third and especially second millennia BC, except for the rather fragmentary insights mainly provided by Egyptian textual evidence (Moreno García 2018). While quite a lot of data are available on the Egyptian and Greek-Roman activities in the Eastern Desert, we have scarce evidence of the local inhabitants of this vast region: few insights are available on these peoples, mainly for the phases in which, for different reasons, in the first half of the second millennium BC and around the mid-first millennium AD, they were more intensively interacting with the Nile valley (Sections 2.2, 2.6). In the case of the inland regions to the west and east of the Nile valley, scarce explorations are perhaps due to the lack of monumental sites, which are, lamentably, often regarded as the sole markers of the presence of highly structured social organizations (Edwards 2003: 138). The limited adoption in these areas of intensive – rather than extensive – survey strategies aimed at investigating the evanescent remains that a temporary camp may leave (Wendrich & Barnard 2008: 11–13) also explains this gap in our knowledge. Moreover, the often unconscious prejudice towards areas traditionally inhabited by scarce and nomadic groups of herders survives among the scholars (Edwards 2003: 130–2; Wengrow 2003: 130–1). Nevertheless, it was certainly in those areas that the experiments leading to important innovations took place in the first half of the Holocene (Sections 2.1, 3.3), and the groups inhabiting those remote regions may have played a very relevant role in later phases of history as well (see e.g. Manzo 2020b: 111). Finally, it should be stressed that for the southern fringes of the broad region we were dealing with as well, corresponding to northern Ethiopia and Eritrea, virtually nothing is known of the local cultures before the first millennium BC. Further research is also needed to fill this gap in our present knowledge.

It is therefore certain that in the coming years, as soon as exploration in those areas intensifies, new aspects of the intense relations between Egypt and its African neighbours will emerge. Moreover, similar to the case of other African contexts (see e.g. McIntosh 1999), distinctive and specific paths to social complexity will perhaps be outlined for those regions. Potentially, these studies may also enrich the scholarly perspective on the origins and trajectories of the Egyptian state itself, as sometimes these appear distinctive and original, if compared to the ones of the earliest Near Eastern states (Smith 2018: 339; Wengrow 2003: 125, 129–30). Indeed, it is undeniable that Egyptian state, society and culture are traditionally placed within a Near Eastern interpretative framework, but they unquestionably emerged and developed between the Near East, the Mediterranean and Africa, as a result of being rooted in the northernmost sector of the valley of Africa's longest river.

Indeed, I feel that in the near future a specific issue that could potentially provide new data is that pertaining to the contributions of Egypt's African neighbours to Egyptian culture and civilization through mutual contact and exchange (Section 3.3). For two main reasons I believe that we have only scratched the surface in this field. Firstly, the aforementioned scarce archaeo-logical knowledge of several of the African neighbours of Egypt means that we may have much to uncover on their contributions to the Egyptian culture. Secondly, the ideological, often unconscious, prejudice to recognize African contributions to Egyptian culture is an enduring impediment. Therefore, if the contribution of Egypt to the cultures of its neighbours is certain and cannot be put to discussion, a lot of work remains to be done to identify any African elements that were embedded in Egyptian culture throughout history. Of course, in the case of both Egypt and its African neighbours, the task is also to undertake an in-depth investigation of the reasons leading to the adoption of foreign elements and of the new meanings that were awarded to cultural traits across the various contexts (see also Smith 2018: 338; Török 2018: 2). Indeed, if it is evident that sometimes the origin of cultural traits in Egypt and in its African neighbours was ultimately exogenous, the factors behind the specific selection of these traits out of all the possible exogenous elements that could be adopted also requires investigation and explanation, as well as their adaptation to the new context. In the years to follow, the investigation of all these challenging issues will certainly greatly enrich our knowledge of ancient Egypt, its African neighbours and their interactions in their wider African setting.

# References

Adams, W. Y. (1977). *Nubia: Corridor to Africa*. London: Allen Lane.

Anderson, J. R., and Welsby, D. A., eds. (2004). *Sudan Ancient Treasures*. London: The British Museum Press.

Andrews, C. (1990). *Ancient Egyptian Jewellery*. London: The British Museum Press.

Bard, K. A., and Fattovich, R. (2018). *Seafaring Expeditions to Punt in the Middle Kingdom. Excavations at Mersa/Wadi Gawasis. Egypt*. Leiden/ Boston: Brill.

Bárta, M. (2018). The Birth of Supernatural. On the Genesis of Some Later Ancient Egyptian Concepts. In J. Kabaciński, M. Chłodnicki, M. Kobusiewicz and M. Winiarska-Kabacińska, eds. *Desert and the Nile. Prehistory of the Nile Basin and the Sahara Papers in Honour of Fred Wendorf*. Poznań: Poznań Archaeological Museum, 669–85.

Binder, S. (2008). *The Gold of Honour in the New Kingdom Egypt*. Oxford: Aris and Phillips Ltd.

Blackman, A. M. (1914). *The Rock Tombs of Meir*, vol. 1, *The Tomb-Chapel of Ueh-hotp's Son Senbi*. London: Egypt Exploration Fund.

Bonnet, Ch. (2000). *Édifices et rites funéraires à Kerma*. Paris: Errance.

Bonnet, Ch. (2004). *Le temple principal de la ville de Kerma et son quartier religieux*. Paris: Errance.

Bonnet, Ch. (2008). L'occupation égyptienne du Nouvel Empire à Doukki Gel. L'apport de l'archéologie. In W. Godlewski and A. Łajtar, eds. *Between the Cataracts. Proceedings of the 11th Conference of Nubian Studies*, vol. 1. Warsaw: Warsaw University Press, 75–84.

Bonnet, Ch. (2014). *La ville de Kerma. Une capitale nubienne au sud de l'Égypte*. Paris: Favre.

Bonnet, Ch. , and Valbelle, D. (2003). Un dépôt de statues royales du début du VIe siècle av. J.-C. à Kerma. *Comptes rendus de l'Académie des Inscriptions et Belles-Lettres*, 747–69.

Brass, M. (2018). Early North African Cattle Domestication and Its Ecological Setting: A Reassessment. *Journal of World Prehistory*, 31, 81–115.

Breyer, F. (2016). *Punt: die Suche nach dem 'Gottesland'*. Leiden/Boston: Brill.

Burstein, S. M., ed., tr. (1989). *Agatharchides of Cnidus, On the Erythrean Sea*. London: Hakluyt Society.

Casson, L., ed., tr. (1989). *The Periplus Maris Erythraei. Text with Introduction, Translation, and Commentary*. Princeton: Princeton University Press.

Casson, L. (1993). Ptolemy II and the Hunting of African Elephants. *Transactions of the American Philological Association*, 123, 247–60.

Cervelló Autori, J. (1996). *Egipto y África. Origen de la civilización y la monarqía faraónicas en su contexto africano*. Barcelona: AUSA.

Červiček, P. (1986). *Rock Pictures of Upper Egypt and Nubia*. Naples: Istituto Universitario Orientale.

Clayton, J., de Trafford, A., and Borda, M. (2008). A Hieroglyphic Inscription Found at Jebel Uweinat Mentioning Yam and Tekhebet. *Sahara*, 19, 129–34.

Cooper, J. (2012). Reconsidering the Location of Yam. *Journal of the American Research Center in Egypt*, 48, 1–21.

Darnell, J. C. (2003). The Rock Inscriptions of Tjehemau at Abisko. *Zeitschrift für ägyptische Sprache*, 130, 31–48.

Darnell, J. C. (2006). *The Inscription of Queen Katimala at Semna: Textual Evidence for the Origins of the Napatan State*. New Haven: Yale University.

Darnell, J. C. (2007). The Deserts. In T. Wilkinson (ed.), *The Egyptian World*. London and New York: Routledge, 29–48.

Davies, V. W. (2003). Kush in Egypt: A New Historical Inscription. *Sudan & Nubia*, 7, 52–4.

Davies, V. W. (2014). Recording Egyptian Inscriptions in the Desert and Elsewhere. *Sudan & Nubia*, 18, 30–44.

Davies, V. W. (2017). Nubia in the New Kingdom: The Egyptians at Kurgus. In N. Spencer, A. Stevens and M. Binder, eds. *Nubia in the New Kingdom. Lived Experience, Pharaonic Control and Indigenous Traditions*. Leuven/Paris/Bristol: Peeters, 65–105.

Davies, N., and Gardiner, A. (1926). *The Tomb of Huy, Viceroy of Nubia in the Reign of Tutankhamun (No. 40)*. London: Egypt Exploration Society.

Deichmann, F. W. (1966). Eine alabasterne Largitionsschale aus Nubien. In W. N. Schumacher, ed. *Tortulae. Studien zu altchristlichen und byzantinischen Monumenten*. Rom-Freiburg-Wien: Herder, 65–76.

de Souza, A. (2018). *New Horizons: The Pan-Grave Ceramic Tradition in Context*. London: Golden House Publications.

de Souza, A. (2020). Melting Pots: Entanglement, Appropriation, Hybridity, and Assertive Objects between the Pan-Grave and Egyptian Ceramic Traditions. *Journal of Ancient Egyptian Interconnections*, 27, 1–23.

Dumont, H. J. (2009). A Description of the Nile Basin, and a Synopsis of Its History, Ecology, Biogeography, Hydrology, and Natural Resources. In H. J. Dumont, ed. *The Nile. Origin, Environments, Limnology and Human Use*. Heidelberg: Springer, 1–21.

Edwards, D. N. (1996). *The Archaeology of the Meroitic State. New Perspectives on Its Social and Political Organisation*. Oxford: Tempus Reparatum.

Edwards, D. N. (2003). Ancient Egypt in the Sudanese Middle Nile: A Case of Mistaken Identity?. In D. O'Connor and A. Reid, eds. *Ancient Egypt in Africa*. Walnut Creek: Left Coast Press, 137–50.

Edwards, D. N. (2004). *The Nubian Past: An Archaeology of the Sudan*. London: Routledge.

Eide, T., Hägg, T., Pierce, R. H., and Török, L., eds. (1994). *Fontes Historiae Nubiorum*, vol. 1, *From the Eighth to the mid-Fifth Century BC*. Bergen: Universitetet i Bergen.

Eide, T., Hägg, T., Pierce, R. H., and Török, L., eds. (1998). *Fontes Historiae Nubiorum*, vol. 3, *From the First to the Sixth Century AD*. Bergen: Universitetet i Bergen.

Ejsmond, W. (2019). Some Thoughts on Nubians in Gebelein Region during First Intermediate Period. In M. Peterková Hlouchová, D. Belohoubková, J. Honzl and V. Nováková, eds. *Current Research in Egyptology 2018*. Oxford: Archaeopress, 23–41.

Emberling, G., and Williams, B. (2010). The Kingdom of Kush in the 4th Cataract: Archaeological Salvage of the Oriental Institute Nubian Expedition 2007 Season. Part I. Preliminary Report on the Sites of Hosh el-Guruf and El-Widay. *Gdańsk Archaeological Museum African Reports*, 7, 17–38.

Emery, W. B., Smith, H. S., and Millard, A. (1979). *The Fortress of Buhen 1. The Archaeological Report*. London: Egypt Exploration Society.

Espinel, A. D. (2011). *Abriendo los caminos de Punt. Contactos entre Egipto y el ámbito afroárabe durante la Edad del Bronce [ca. 3000 a.C.–1065 a.C.]*. Barcelona: Bellaterra arquelogía.

Firth, C. M. (1927). *The Archaeological Survey of Nubia. Report for 1910–1911*. Cairo: Government Press.

Fischer, H. G. (1961). The Nubian Mercenaries of Gebelein during the First Intermediate Period. *Kush*, 9, 44–81.

Fischer, H. G. (1963). Varia Aegyptiaca. *Journal of the American Research Center in Egypt*, 2, 15–51.

Förster, F. (2013). Beyond Dakhla: The Abu Ballas Trail in the Libyan Desert (SW Egypt). In F. Förster and H. Reimer, eds. *Desert Road Archaeology in Ancient Egypt and Beyond*. Köln: Heinrich-Barth-Institut, 297–333.

Frankfort, H. (1948). *Kingship and the Gods. A Study of Ancient Near Eastern Religion as Integration of Society and Nature*. Chicago/London: University of Chicago Press.

Friedman, R. (2001). Nubians at Hierakonpolis. Excavations in the Nubian Cemeteries. *Sudan & Nubia*, 5, 29–38.

Friedman, R., and Hobbs, J. J. (2002). A 'Tasian' Tomb in Egypt's Eastern Desert. In R. Friedman, ed. *Egypt and Nubia. Gifts of the Desert*. London: The British Museum Press, 178–91.

Gabolde, L. (2003). La stele de Thoutmosis II à Assouan, témoin historique et archetype littéraire. *Orientalia Monspeliensa*, 14, 129–48.

Gatto, M. C. (2006). The Nubian A-Group: A Reassessment. *Archéo-Nil*, 16, 61–76.

Gatto, M. C. (2009). Egypt and Nubia in the 5th–4th Millennia BCE: A View from the First Cataract and Its Surroundings. *British Museum Studies in Ancient Egypt and Sudan*, 13, 125–45.

Gatto, M. C. (2011). The Nubian Pastoral Culture as Link between Egypt and Africa: A View from the Archaeological Record. In K. Exell (ed.), *Egypt in Its African Context: Proceedings of the Conference Held at the Manchester Museum, University of Manchester, 2–4 October 2009*. Oxford: Archaeopress, 21–9.

Gatto, M. C., and Zerboni, A. (2015). Holocene Supra-Regional Environmental Changes as Trigger for Major Socio-Cultural Processes in Northeastern Africa and the Sahara. *African Archaeological Review*, 32, 301–33.

Giuliani, S. (2001). Pottery from the Nubian Cemeteries. *Sudan & Nubia*, 5, 40–5.

Gratien, B. (1978). *Les cultures Kerma. Essai de classification*. Lille: Publications de l'Université de Lille III.

Hasfaas, H. (2005). *Cattle Pastoralists in a Multicultural Setting. The C-Group People in Lower Nubia*. Bergen: Center for Development Studies–Bergen University.

Hatke, G. (2013). *Aksum and Nubia. Warfare, Commerce, and Political Fictions in Ancient Northeast Africa*. New York: New York University Press–Institute for the Study of the Ancient World.

Heidorn, Lisa A. (1994). Historical Implications of the Pottery from the Earliest Tombs at El Kurru. *Journal of the American Research Center in Egypt*, 31, 115–31.

Hintze, F. (1959). Preliminary Report of the Butana Expedition. *Kush*, 7, 171–96.

Honegger, M. (2014). *Aux origines des pharaons noirs. 10.000 ans d'archéologie en Nubie*. Hauterive: Laténium–Fondation Kerma.

Honegger, M. (2018). La plus ancienne tombe royale du royaume de Kerma en Nubie. *Bulletin de la Société neuchâteloise des sciences naturelles*, 138, 185–98.

Hope, C. (2002). Early and Mid-Holocene Ceramics from the Dakhleh Oasis: Traditions and Influences. In R. Friedman (ed.), *Egypt and Nubia. Gifts of the Desert*. London: The British Museum Press, 39–61.

Jesse, F. (2013). Far from the Nile – The Gala Abu Ahmed Fortress in the Lower Wadi Howar (Northern Sudan). In F. Jesse and C. Vogel, eds. *The Power of Walls: Fortifications in Ancient Northeastern Africa*. Köln: Heinrich-Barth-Institut, 321–2.

Jesse, F., Kröpelin, S., Lange, M., Pöllath, N., and Berke, H. (2004). On the periphery of Kerma: The Handessi Horizon in the Wadi Hariq, Northwestern Sudan. *Journal of African Archaeology*, 2, 123–64.

Jiménez-Serrano, A. (2006). Two Different Names of Nubia before the Fifth Dynasty. *Studien zur Altägyptischen Kultur*, 35, 141–5.

Kanawati, N. (2017). Ritual Marriage Alliances and Consolidation of Power in Middle Egypt during the Middle Kingdom. *Études et Travaux*, 30, 267–88.

Kaper, O. E., and Willems, H. (2002). Policing the Desert: Old Kingdom Activity around the Dakhleh Oasis. In R. Friedman, ed. *Egypt and Nubia. Gifts of the Desert*. London: The British Museum Press, 79–94.

Kemp, B. J. (1972). Fortified Towns in Nubia. In P. J. Ucko, R. Tringham and G. W. Dimbleby, eds. *Man, Settlement and Urbanism*. London: Duckworth, 651–6.

Kendall, T. (1997). *Kerma and the Kingdom of Kush 2500–1500 BC. The Archaeological Discovery of an Ancient Nubian Empire*. Washington, DC: National Museum of African Art.

Kendall, T. (1999). The Origin of the Napatan State: El Kurru and the Evidence for the Royal Ancestors. In S. Wenig, ed. *Studien zum antiken Sudan. Akten der 7. Internationalen Tagung für meroitische Forschungen*. Wiesbaden: Otto Harrassowitz, 3–117.

Klotz, D. (2015). Darius I and the Sabaeans: Ancient Partners in Red Sea Navigation. *Journal of Near Eastern Studies*, 74, 267–80.

Kuper, R. (2002). Routes and Roots in Egypt's Western Desert: The Early Holocene Resettlement of the Eastern Sahara. In R. Friedman, ed. *Egypt and Nubia. Gifts of the Desert*. London: The British Museum Press, 1–12.

Łajtar, A., and van der Vliet, J. (2006). The Southernmost Latin Inscription Rediscovered ('CIL' III 83). *Zeitschrift für Papyrologie und Epigraphik*, 157, 193–8.

Lepsius, K. R. (1849). *Denkmäler aus Ägypten und Äthiopien nach den Zeichnungen der von Seiner Majestät dem Könige von Preussen, Friedrich Wilhelm IV., nach diesen Ländern gesendeten, und in den Jahren 1842–1845 ausgeführten wissenschaftlichen Expedition auf Befehl Seiner Majestät*. Berlin: Nicolaische Buchhandlung.

Lichtheim, M. (1988). *Ancient Egyptian Autobiographies Chiefly of the Middle Kingdom*. Freiburg: Universität Verlag.

Liszka, K., and de Souza, A. (2020). Pan-Grave and Medjay. At the Intersection of Archaeology and History. In G. Emberling and B. B. Williams, eds. *The Oxford Handbook of Ancient Nubia*. Oxford: Oxford University Press, 227–49.

Liverani, M. (1990). *Prestige and Interest. International Relations in the Near East ca. 1600–1100 B.C.* Padova: Sargon.

Lloyd, A. B. (1977). Necho and the Red Sea: Some Considerations. *The Journal of Egyptian Archaeology*, 63, 142–55.

Loprieno, A. (1988). *Topos und Mimesis: zum Ausländer in der ägyptischen Literatur*. Wiesbaden: Otto Harrassowitz.

Lowhasser, A. (2001). Queenship in Kush: Status, Role and Ideology of Royal Women. *Journal of the American Research Center in Egypt*, 38, 61–76.

Macadam, L. M. F. (1949). *The Temples of Kawa. The Inscriptions*. Oxford: The Griffith Institute-Ashmolean Museum.

Manzo, A. (1998). The Dynamics of External Contacts of Northern Ethiopia and Eritrea from Proto-Historical to Aksumite Times, Late 2nd Millennium BC-Late 1st Millennium AD. In *Orbis Aethiopicus. Ethiopia and Its Neighbours*. Frankfurt: Muzeum Archeologiczne w Gdańsku-Orbis Aethiopicus, 35–52.

Manzo, A. (1999). *Échanges et contacts le long du Nil et de la Mer Rouge dans l'époque protohistorique (IIIe et IIe millénaires avant J.-C.)*. Oxford: Archaeopress.

Manzo, A. (2003). Skeuomorphism in Aksumite Pottery? Remarks on the Origins and Meanings of Some Ceramic Types. *Æthiopica*, 6, 7–46.

Manzo, A. (2005). Aksumite Trade and the Red Sea Exchange Network: A View from Bieta Giyorgis (Aksum). In J. Starkey, ed. *People of the Red Sea: Proceedings of Red Sea Project 2 Held in the British Museum, October 2004*. Oxford: Archaeopress, 51–66.

Manzo, A. (2006). Apedemak and Dionysos. Further Remarks on the 'Cult of Wine' in Kush. *Sudan & Nubia*, 10, 82–94.

Manzo, A. (2010). Exotic Ceramic Materials from Mersa Gawasis, Red Sea, Egypt. In W. Godlewski and A. Łajtar, eds. *Between the Cataracts. Proceedings of the 11th Conference of Nubian Studies*, vol. 2.2. Warsaw: Warsaw University Press, 439–53.

Manzo, A. (2012). From the Sea to the Deserts and Back: New Research in Eastern Sudan. *British Museum Studies on Ancient Egypt and Sudan*, 18, 75–106.

Manzo, A. (2013). Skeuomorphism in Meroitic Pottery. A Tentative Interpretative Approach. *Rivista degli Studi Orientali*, 85, 339–72.

Manzo, A. (2016). Weapons, Ideology and Identity at Kerma (Upper Nubia, 2500–1500 BC). *Annali Istituto Universitario Orientale Napoli*, 76, 3–29.

Manzo, A. (2020a). Back to Mahal Teglinos: New Pharaonic Evidence from Eastern Sudan. *The Journal of Egyptian Archaeology*, 106, 1–16.

Manzo, A. (2020b). Clash of Civilisations on the First Cataract? A Southern Point of View, from Old Assumptions to New Complexities. *Ägypten und Levante*, 30, 101–13.

McIntosh, S. K. (1999). Pathways to Complexity: An African Perspective. In S. K. McIntosh, ed. *Beyond Chiefdoms: Pathways to Complexity in Africa*. Cambridge: Cambridge University Press, 1–30.

Moreno García, J. C. (2018). Elusive 'Libyans': Identities, Lifestyles and Mobile Populations in NE Africa (late 4th-early 2nd millennium BCE). *Journal of Egyptian History*, 11, 147–84.

Morkot, R. (1991). Nubia and Achaemenid Persia: Sources and Problems. In H. Sancisi-Weerdenburg and A. Kuhrt, eds. *Achaemenid History VI. Asia Minor and Egypt: Old Cultures in a New Empire*. Leiden: Nederlands Instituut voor het Nabije Oosten, 321–36.

Morkot, R. (2000). *The Black Pharaohs: Egypt's Nubian Rulers*. London: The Rubicon.

Morkot, R. (2007). Tradition, Innovation and Researching the Past in Libyan, Kushite and Saïte Egypt. In H. Crawford, ed. *Regime Change in Ancient Near East and Egypt: From Sargon of Agade to Saddam Hussein*. Oxford: Oxford University Press, 141–64.

Morkot, R. (2013). From Conquered to Conqueror: The Organization of Nubia in the New Kingdom and the Kushite Administration of Egypt. In J. C. Moreno García, ed. *Ancient Egyptian Administration*. Leiden/Boston: Brill, 911–63.

Morkot, R. (2016a). Before Greeks and Romans. Eastern Libya and the Oases: A Brief Review of Interconnections in the Eastern Sahara. In N. Mugnai, J. Nikolaus and N. Ray, eds. *De Africa Romaque: Merging Cultures across North Africa*. London: Society for Libyan Studies, 27–38.

Morkot, R. (2016b). North-east Africa and Trade at the Crossroads of the Nile valley, the Mediterranean and the Red Sea. In J. C. Moreno García, ed. *Dynamics of Production in the Ancient Near East 1300–500 BC*. Oxford/Philadelphia: Oxbow, 257–74.

Obsomer, C. (2007). Les expeditions d'Herkouf (VI$^e$ dynastie) et la localisation de Iam. In M.-C. Bruwier, ed. *Pharaons noirs. Sur la Piste des Quarante Jours*. Mariemont: Musée Royal de Mariemont, 39–52.

O'Connor, D. (1987). The Location of Irem. *The Journal of Egyptian Archaeology*, 73, 99–136.

O'Connor, D. (2014). *The Old Kingdom Town at Buhen*. London: Egypt Exploration Society.

O'Connor, D., and Reid, D. (2003). Introduction – Locating Ancient Egypt in Africa: Modern Theories, Past Realities. In D. O'Connor and A. Reid, eds., *Ancient Egypt in Africa*. Walnut Creek: Left Coast Press-UCL, 1–22.

Osing, J. (1976). Ächtungstexte aus dem Alten Reich (II). *Mitteilungen des Deutschen Archäologischen Instituts Abteilung Kairo*, 32, 133–85.

Osman, A., and Edwards, D. N. (2012). *The Archaeology of a Nubian Frontier. Survey on the Nile Third Cataract, Sudan*. Bristol: Mauhaus.

Panagiotopoulos, D. (2006). Foreigners in Egypt in the Time of Hatshepsut and Thutmose III. In E. H. Cline and D. O'Connor, eds., *Thutmose III. A New Biography*. Ann Arbor: University of Michigan Press, 370–412.

Petrie, W. M. F. (1920). *Prehistoric Egypt*. London: British School of Archaeology in Egypt-University College.

Phillipson, D. W. (2012). *Foundations of an African Civilisation. Aksum & the Northern Horn 1000 BC–AD 1300*. Woodbridge: James Currey.

Piacentini, P. (1990). *L'autobiografia di Uni, Principe e Governatore dell'alto Egitto*. Pisa: Giardini.

Raue, D. (2019). *Elephantine und Nubien vom 4.-2. Jahrtausend v.Chr.* Berlin: de Gruyter.

Reid, M. (2003). Ancient Egypt and the Source of the Nile. In D. O'Connor and A. Reid, eds., *Ancient Egypt in Africa*. Walnut Creek: Left Coast Press/UCL, 55–76.

Reisner, G. A. (1923a). *Excavations at Kerma. Parts I-III. Harvard, MA*: Peabody Museum of Harvard University.

Reisner, G. A. (1923b). *Excavations at Kerma. Parts IV-V*, Harvard MA: Peabody Museum of Harvard University.

Riemer, H., and Kindermann, K. (2019). Eastern Saharan Prehistory during the 9th to 5th Millennium BC. The View from the 'Libyan Desert'. In D. Raue, ed., *Handbook of Ancient Nubia*, vol. 1. Berlin/Boston: De Gruyter, 195–216.

Rilly, C. (2007). *La langue du royaume de Méroé. Un panorama de la plus ancienne culture écrite d'Afrique subsaharienne*. Paris: Honoré Champion Éditeur.

Roehrig, C. H. (ed.) (2005). *Hatshepsut from Queen to Pharaoh*. New York/New Haven, CT/London: The Metropolitan Museum of Art/Yale University Press.

Rowley-Conwy, P. (1988). The Camel in the Nile Valley: New Radiocarbon Accelerator (AMS) Dates from Qaṣr Ibrim. *The Journal of Egyptian Archaeology*, 74, 245–8.

Ryholt, K. (2018). Seals and History of the 14th and 15th Dynasties. In I. Forstner-Müller and N. Moeller, eds., *The Hyksos Ruler Khyan and the Early Second Intermediate Period in Egypt: Problems and Priorities of Current Research.* Vienna: Österreichischen Akademie der Wissenschaften, 235–76.

Rzeuska, T. (2010). Zigzag, Triangle and Fish Fin. On the Relations of Egypt and C-Group during the Middle Kingdom. In W. Godlewski and A. Łajtar, eds., *Between the Cataracts. Proceedings of the 11th Conference of Nubian Studies*, vol. 2.2. Warsaw: Warsaw University Press, 397–419.

Sadr, K. (1997). The Wadi Elei Finds: Nubian Desert Gold Mining in the 5th and 4th Millennia BC?. *Cahier de Recherches de l'Institut de Papyrologie et d'Égyptologie de Lille*, 17/2, 67–76.

Salvatori, S., and Usai, D. (2019). The Neolithic and 'Pastoralism' Along the Nile: A Dissenting View. *Journal of World Prehistory*, 32, 251–85.

Scullard, H. H. (1974). *The Elephant in the Greek and Roman World*. London: Thames & Hudson.

Seidlmayer, S. H. (2002). Nubier im ägyptischen Kontext im Alten und Mittleren Reich. In S. Leder and B. Streck, eds., *Akkulturation und Selbstbehauptung*. Halle: OWZ Martin-Luther-Universität, 89–113.

Sidebotham, S. E. (1986). *Roman Economic Policy in the Erythra Thalassa, 30 BC–AD 217*. Leiden: Brill.

Smith, H. S., and Smith, A. (1976). A Reconsideration of the Kamose Texts. *Zeitschrift für ägyptische Sprache und Altertumskunde*, 103, 48–76.

Smith, S. T. (2003). *Wretched Kush: Ethnic Identities and Boundaries in Egypt's Nubian Empire*. London: Routledge.

Smith, S. T. (2014). Editorial Essay: Nubia, Coming Out of the Shadow of Egypt. *Journal of Ancient Egyptian Interconnections*, 6, 1–4.

Smith, S. T. (2018). Gift of the Nile? Climate Change, the Origins of Egyptian Civilization and Its Interactions within Northeast Africa. In T.A. Bács, Á. Bollók and T. Vida, eds., *Across the Mediterranean – Along the Nile. Studies in Egyptology, Nubiology and Late Antiquity Dedicated to László Török on the Occasion of His 75th Birthday*, vol. 1. Budapest: Institute of Archaeology, Research Centre for the Humanities, Hungarian Academy of Sciences/Museum of Fine Arts Budapest, 325–45.

Smither, P. C. (1945). The Semnah Despatches. *The Journal of Egyptian Archaeology*, 31, 3–10.

Snape, S. (2013). A Stroll along the Corniche? Coastal Routes between the Nile Delta and Cyrenaica in the Late Bronze Age. In F. Förster and H. Reimer, eds., *Desert Road Archaeology in Ancient Egypt and Beyond*. Cologne: Heinrich-Barth-Institut, 439–54.

Takamiya, I. H. (2004). Egyptian Pottery Distribution in A-Group Cemeteries, Lower Nubia: Towards an Understanding of Exchange Systems between the Naqada Culture and the A-Group. *The Journal of Egyptian Archaeology*, 90, 35–62.

Torcia, M. (2020). *Creatulae: A Basic Class of Objects in the Archaeological Research (Pre- Early-Dynastic/Old Kingdom periods)*. Baeau Bassin: Lap Lambert Academic Publishing.

Török, L. (1988). *Late Antique Nubia*. Budapest: Archaeological Institute of the Hungarian Academy of Sciences.

Török, L. (1989). Kush and the External World. In S. Donadoni and S. Wenig, eds., *Studia Meroitica 1984: Proceedings of the Fifth International Conference for Meroitic Studies*. Berlin: Akademie-Verlag, 49–215.

Török, L. (1989–1990). Augustus and Meroe. *Orientalia Suecana*, 38–9, 171–90.

Török, L. (1997). *The Kingdom of Kush. Handbook of the Napatan-Meroitic Civilization*. Leiden: Brill.

Török, L. (2002). *The Image of the Ordered World in Ancient Nubian Art. The Construction of the Kushite Mind (800 BC-300 AD)*. Leiden/Boston/Cologne: Brill.

Török, L. (2009). *Between Two Worlds. The Frontier Region between Ancient Nubia and Egypt 3700 BC–AD 500*. Leiden: Brill.

Török, L. (2011). *Hellenizing Art in Ancient Nubia 300 BC–AD 250. A Study in 'Acculturation'*, Leiden/Boston: Brill.

Török, L. (2018). Nubians Move from the Margins to the Center of Their History. In P. Steiner, A. Tsakos and E. Heldaas Seland, eds., *From the Fjords to the Nile. Essays in honour of Richard Holton Pierce on His 80th Birthday*. Oxford: Archaeopress, 1–18.

Trigger, B. G. (1987). Egypt: A Fledgling Nation. *Journal of the Society for the Study of Egyptian Antiquities*, 17, 58–66.

Trigger, B. G. (1994). Paradigms in Sudan Archaeology. *Journal of African History*, 27, 323–45.

Valbelle, D. (2004). The Cultural Significance of Iconographic and Epigraphic Data Found in the Kingdom of Kerma. In T. Kendall, ed., *Nubian Studies 1998. Proceedings of the Ninth Conference of the International Society of Nubian Studies*. Boston: Northeastern University, 176–83.

Valbelle, D. (2011). Les statues égyptiennes découvertes à Kerma et Doukki Gel. In D. Valbelle and J.-M. Yoyotte, eds., *Statues égyptiennes et kouchites démembrées et reconstituées*. Paris: Presses de l'Université Paris-Sorbonne, 13–20.

Vercoutter, J. (1962). Un Palais des 'Candaces' contemporain d'Auguste. (Fouilles de Wad-ban-Naga 1958–1960). *Syria*, 39, 263–99.

Vermeersch, P. M., Linseele, V., Marinova, E., van Neer, W., Moeyersons, J., and Rethemeyer, J. (2015). Early and Middle Holocene Human Occupation of the Egyptian Eastern Desert: Sodmein Cave. *African Archaeological Review*, 32, 465–503.

Vincentelli, I. (2006). *Hillat el-Arab: The Joint Sudanese–Italian Expedition in the Napatan Region, Sudan*. Oxford: Archeopress.

Vincentelli, I. (2006–7). Some Clay Sealings from Sanam Abu Dom. In B. Gratien, ed., *Mélanges offerts à Francis Geus*. Lille: Université Charles-de-Gaulle-Lille 3, 371–8.

Vincentelli, I. (2011). The Treasury and Other Buildings at Sanam. In V. Rondot, F. Alpi and F. Villeneuve, eds. *La pioche et la plume. Autour du Soudan, du Liban et de la Jordanie. Hommages archéologiques à Patrice Lenoble*. Paris: Presses de l'Université Paris-Sorbonne, 269–82.

Vogel, C. (2010). *The Fortifications of Ancient Egypt 3000–1780 BC*. Oxford: Osprey.

Voos, S. (2016). Wissenshintergründe . . . – Die Ägyptologie als 'völkische' Wissenschaft entlang des Nachlasses Georg Steindorffs von der Weimarer Republik über die NS- bis zur Nachkriegszeit. In S. Voos and D. Raue, eds., *Georg Steindorff und die deutsche Ägyptologie im 20. Jahrhundert: Wissenshintergründe und Forschungstransfers*. Berlin/Boston: De Gruyter, 105–332.

Wegner, J. (2017–18). The Stela of Idudju-Iker: Foremost One of the Chiefs of Wawat. New Evidence on the Conquest of Thinis under Wahank Antef II. *Revue d'Égytoplogie*, 68, 153–209.

Welsby, D. A. (2002). *The Medieval Kingdoms of Nubia. Pagans, Christians and Muslims along the Middle Nile*. London: The British Museum Press.

Wendorf, F., and Schild, R. (2002). Implications of Incipient Social Complexity in the Late Neolithic in the Egyptian Sahara. In R. Friedman, ed., *Egypt and Nubia. Gifts of the Desert*. London: The British Museum Press, 13–20.

Wendrich, W., and Barnard, H. (2008). The Archaeology of Mobility: Definitions and Research Approaches. In H. Barnard and W. Wendrich, eds., *The Archaeology of Mobility. Old World and New World Nomadism*. Los Angeles: Cotsen Institute of Archaeology/University of California, 1–21.

Wendrich, W., Taylor, R. E., and Southon, J. (2010). Dating Stratified Settlement Sites at Kom K and Kom W: Fifth Millennium BCE Radiocarbon Ages for the Fayum Neolithic. *Nuclear Instruments & Methods in Physics Research, Section B: Beam Interactions with Materials and Atoms*, 268, 999–1002.

Wengrow, D. (2003). Landscapes of Knowledge, Idioms of Power: The African Foundations of Ancient Egyptian Civilization Reconsidered. In D. O'Connor and A. Reid, eds., *Ancient Egypt in Africa*. Walnut Creek: Left Coast Press, 121–35.

Wengrow, D., Dee, M., Foster, S., Stevenson, A., and Bronk Ramsey, C. (2014). Cultural Convergence in the Neolithic of the Nile Valley: A Prehistoric Perspective on Egypt's Place in Africa. *Antiquity*, 88, 95–111.

Williams, B. B. (1986). *The A-Group Royal Cemetery at Qustul: Cemetery L.* Chicago: The Oriental Institute of the University of Chicago.

Winchell, F., Stevens, C. J., Murphy, C., Champion, L., and Fuller, D. Q. (2017). Evidence for Sorghum Domestication in Fourth Millennium BC Eastern Sudan. *Current Anthropology*, 58, 673–83.

# Cambridge Elements ≡

# Ancient Egypt in Context

## Gianluca Miniaci

*University of Pisa*

Gianluca Miniaci is Associate Professor in Egyptology at the University of Pisa, Honorary Researcher at the Institute of Archaeology, UCL – London, and Chercheur associé at the École Pratique des Hautes Études, Paris. He is currently co-director of the archaeological mission at Zawyet Sultan (Menya, Egypt). His main research interest focuses on the social history and the dynamics of material culture in the Middle Bronze Age Egypt and its interconnections between the Levant, Aegean and Nubia.

## Juan Carlos Moreno García

*CNRS, Paris*

Juan Carlos Moreno García (PhD in Egyptology, 1995) is a CNRS senior researcher at the University of Paris IV-Sorbonne, as well as lecturer on social and economic history of ancient Egypt at the École des Hautes Études en Sciences Sociales (EHESS) in Paris. He has published extensively on the administration, socio-economic history and landscape organization of ancient Egypt, usually in a comparative perspective with other civilizations of the ancient world, and has organized several conferences on these topics.

## Anna Stevens

*University of Cambridge and Monash University*

Anna Stevens is a research archaeologist with a particular interest in how material culture and urban space can shed light on the lives of the non-elite in ancient Egypt. She is Senior Research Associate at the McDonald Institute for Archaeological Research and Assistant Director of the Amarna Project (both University of Cambridge).

## About the Series

The aim of this Elements series is to offer authoritative but accessible overviews of foundational and emerging topics in the study of ancient Egypt, along with comparative analyses, translated into a language comprehensible to non-specialists. Its authors will take a step back and connect ancient Egypt to the world around, bringing ancient Egypt to the attention of the broader humanities community and leading Egyptology in new directions.

Cambridge Elements $\equiv$

# Ancient Egypt in Context

## Elements in the Series